SELF-WORKBOOK:

THE ULTIMATE GUIDED PROGRAM FOR PRACTICING SELF-CONFIDENCE AND SELF-CARE. GUIDED ACTIVITIES TO STOP SELF-DOUBT AND INSECURITY TO THRIVE AND GAIN INNER STRENGTH.

© **Copyright 2020 - All rights reserved.**

The content contained within this book may not be reproduced, duplicated or transmitted without direct written permission from the author or the publisher.

Under no circumstances will any blame or legal responsibility be held against the publisher, or author, for any damages, reparation, or monetary loss due to the information contained within this book. Either directly or indirectly.

Legal Notice:

This book is copyright protected. This book is only for personal use. You cannot amend, distribute, sell, use, quote or paraphrase any part, or the content within this book, without the consent of the author or publisher.

Disclaimer Notice:

Please note the information contained within this document is for educational and entertainment purposes only. All effort has been executed to present accurate, up to date, and reliable, complete information. No warranties of any kind are declared or implied. Readers acknowledge that the author is not engaging in the rendering of legal, financial, medical or professional advice. The content within this book has been derived from various sources. Please consult a licensed professional before attempting any techniques outlined in this book.

By reading this document, the reader agrees that under no circumstances is the author responsible for any losses, direct or indirect, which are incurred as a result of the use of information contained within this document, including, but not limited to, errors, omissions, or inaccuracies.

Table of Contents

Introduction

Chapter 1 What is Self-Esteem?

Chapter 2 Self-Worth

Chapter 3 The Importance of Being Self-Confidence

Chapter 4 When Self-Confidence Becomes Too Extreme

Chapter 5 Guided Meditation Script - 20min

Chapter 6 How to Visualize Success and Bring It to Life

Chapter 7 Self-Acceptance Habits That Lead to Improved Wellbeing

Chapter 8 Exercises to Set and Achieve Goals

Chapter 9 How to Develop Charisma

Chapter 10 Positive Thinking

Chapter 11 Believe in Yourself

Chapter 12 Comfort Zones

Chapter 13 Leveraging Your New Self-Esteem

Conclusion

Introduction

With confidence, you can take on the world. It is potent. It is essential. Yet, it is in short supply.

A lack of confidence comes in many forms, and self-doubt often hides behind a façade of what looks like self-confidence and assuredness, but it is only a show.

For many, even with success that others covet, they still feel undeserving of its rewards. For the rest, they never found success because they believed that their own voice would come across as deficient or self-important, so they never left their comfort zone; and therefore, they never challenged themselves or took risks.

For both types of people, potential is lost, and lost again, and again.

Have you been waiting for confidence to arrive, so that you can live a life doing things that matter? Have you accepted your lack of confidence as a part of you? In other words, have you owned it in order to feel better about your days and yourself?

How would your life change if you developed confidence that was genuine and bold? What could you do that you cannot do now? What opportunities would open up to you if you were just a bit more self-assured on a daily basis? What opportunities have already passed you by because of your lack of confidence?

In all, what have you given away, hoping for a miracle that confidence would find you without any work involved?

A cheerful life is yours for the taking. Quit being negative and pitiful constantly. Life should be that way. Life should be a great positive thing. We as a whole realize that life is short, so be upbeat and carry on with the belief that you should live. Love yourself as well as other people. Set objectives in each aspect of your life. And after that simply be upbeat. Regardless of what occurs, search for the great and be cheerful. You can have an upbeat life, so take it as of now.

Love yourself and love other individuals more. Try not to harp on terrible past encounters. Consider the majority of the brilliant things about yourself. It might be elusive beneficial things; however, there must be a considerable number of things. Ask some confided-in family or companions, if need be. In any case, don't be so reproachful of yourself. What might you tell your closest companion if they approached you for such a rundown? Presently consider yourself that way and record a rundown. Get out the rundown at whatever point you begin to contemplate yourself and read the rundown so anyone can hear. Watch how you will to begin to have a glad life. Concentrate on other individuals also. Assist them with trip and you won't concentrate on yourself and your very own issues to such an extent. Search for little and huge approaches to be pleasant and help other individuals out as well.

Set a wide range of goals. Set work, family, love life, otherworldly life, recreational, and wellbeing objectives. Make progress toward balance throughout everyday life, but make sure you don't disregard any zone. Set a deadline and don't surrender until you meet your objectives. Try not to be reluctant to flop either, simply attempt once more. You simply find one route not to succeed, that's it in a nutshell. Continue attempting and you will meet your objectives.

Be sure and happy. The main mystery to a cheerful life is being glad and not pitiful. Everything comes down to the psyche. Did you realize that you could pick what you think about? Indeed, you can be glad, yet it is all up to you. Try not to let outside conditions decide your satisfaction. Life isn't reasonable and terrible things happen constantly. In any case, you can't give those things a chance to remove your bliss. Be glad paying little respect to the conditions. Realize that a light lies ahead and be cheerful about that. Think positive contemplations consistently.

It's my aim to have each book I compose finish up with some move you can make today to put the standards talked about in this book to use in your life.

Chapter 1
What is Self-Esteem?

Self-esteem has seen to be thrown around as an umbrella term to explain people's emotions. When someone's down, some may say, "Wow, that person has a low self-esteem." When an individual is boasting about something that they're really proud of or portrays themselves in an incredibly confident light, others may say, "They're overly confident and should probably humble themselves."

The Oxford dictionary definition states that self-esteem is "confidence in one's own worth or abilities." In reality, however, self-esteem is so much more than that.

Simply speaking, it is a person's perception of their own self-worth. It often outlines what they feel they're worthy of and how entitled they seem to certain aspects of life.

In more specific terminology, self-esteem is the confidence that someone has in themselves and their abilities. It measures many factors that are linked to confidence, such as what they feel they are capable of accomplishing, how they deserve to be treated, how others should perceive them, and what they should be entitled to.

Individuals with low self-esteem will often view themselves in a negative light. They will believe that they are not worth others time and constantly talk down to themselves. Because of that, they tend to shut people out of their lives and begin drifting away from reality, which is a gateway to a number of other issues and conditions such as depression and anxiety.

On the other hand, the people who demonstrate a high sense of self-esteem are often viewed as extremely confident and outspoken individuals. They are the types who are not afraid to raise their voice and make their opinions heard. They feel like they are worth other people's time and will not hesitate to go out and get what they truly want because they assume that they deserve it.

When you suffer from low self-esteem, you may idolize individuals who find themselves on the opposite side of the spectrum. When you feel the opposite, you may not understand why some other people don't just "feel the same" or stop sulking in their own self-pity. The reality of the whole situation, however, is a lot more complex than that. This book will hopefully give you a better understanding of how self-esteem works and help you identify where you are personally.

What Affects Self-Esteem

Self-esteem is a very tricky thing to look into. Seeing that it's a totally neuro-related concept (meaning, it's quite literally all in your head) that is hard to detect and deal with using machines and modern technology, there is not a lot we can say from a strictly scientific point of view.

We can, however, slowly get into someone's head using social skills and tricks such as therapy. With this information, we can better understand someone and grasp a better concept of their history as a person. From here, we can find what may have triggered an individual to display signs of low or high self-esteem and help them get on a better path.

For the past hundreds of years, doctors, therapists, and social workers alike have been able to compile some of the patterns that are seen between patients and come up with some reasons as to why some people suffer from very low self-esteem while others seem to thrive and love every part of their body.

Thanks to modern medicine and the access to the information that we have now, we're able to publish these results to the world and (hopefully) teach them something about the people and world around them. This is where we have learned what affects self-esteem.

Listed below are the top **six** things that scientists believe affect self-esteem (both negatively and positively). It's important to take note that these may not all apply to you. Everyone is different and trying to compare your life experiences and self-esteem to someone else's is an almost guaranteed way to lower your self-confidence and sabotage your plan to start believing in yourself.

How You Were Raised

The way we were raised as kids has one of the largest impacts on our self-esteem. As toddlers, young kids, and teenagers, we're very vulnerable to the support and lifestyle of the people around us. Take a kid and put them into a household where they're forced to fight for food and work for 16 hours a day to get by, and you'll see how they may not feel like they're worth all that much.

On the other hand, if you were to place a child into a home that has two loving parents who want the best for their kids while still letting them live their best lives, you may observe that this person has a higher self-esteem and believes in their abilities a little more than the other, less-advantaged kid.

When we're growing up, positive reinforcement and praise are essential. Because we are so vulnerable at such a young age, our sense of belonging and love begin to act as the foundation for our future selves. This is why numerous scientists suggest that human interaction and affection (such as hugs, friendly kisses, or "vent-sessions") are some of the most important building blocks when developing a child's self-esteem and sense of worth.

The People You Surround Yourself With

A large chunk of how you feel about yourself comes from the people you're with during your day-to-day activities. The way people interact with you, the way you interact with them, and the connections you have with these people will determine how you may view yourself.

Think about it this way: if you're constantly surrounded by people who help you through your rough patches, make sure you're okay, and celebrate your biggest accomplishments, how do you think you'd feel? Now imagine you're surrounded by people who only seem to talk to you because they feel like it's an obligation and don't really care about what you're saying. Or maybe they're only free when it benefits them, and they don't ever seem to make room for you in their daily schedules. How do you think you'd feel in that scenario?

Odds are, the first one would make you feel like you're worthy and more confident in your abilities to be around others. You're surrounded by people who genuinely care and are okay with seeing the darker side of you. In a sense, they are *validating* your existence. The second scenario, on the other hand, may have you questioning your connections with such individuals. "Why don't they like me?" "Why don't they make time for me?" "What am I doing wrong that is making them not want to be around me?" These are the kind of things that we tend to ask ourselves in one-way relationships. Over time, the same questions will start to have a negative impact on our self-esteem and confidence.

Your Personality

In some cases, your self-esteem may be the direct result of your personality. Understanding who you are at the core may help you see how you just may be someone with low self-esteem.

A good example of this is the perfectionists. These are the kinds of people who need to do *everything* perfectly and won't stop until they're 100% satisfied with the end result. While it can have its advantages, it can also have a plethora of negative drawbacks.

When a perfectionist completes a task, it is rare for them to say, "This is perfect" because perfection is nearly impossible in the real world. Still, they will always find a flaw in their work and highlight it while showing little regard for the quality of the work they actually did. They'll begin to ask themselves, "Why couldn't I do this better?" "How could I not notice this 'huge' flaw?" "What is the point of working on projects like this if I can't even get it right?"

Similar to how someone's self-esteem may suffer around a negative group of people, a perfectionist will suffer from their negative outlook on life and the numerous projects they've accomplished.

Your Hobbies

In some cases, your hobbies might be causing a decline in your self-esteem and self-confidence. While this isn't usually the case for more relaxed and internal hobbies (like making models, drawing, or playing an instrument for fun), it can be a huge hit to your self-esteem when it comes to more 'flashy' hobbies, especially during the beginning stages.

An example of this could be dancing. Assume you've never gone dancing before, but you've always dreamed of it. You go to a dance club, sign up, and get put into a class with 20 other people. They all seem like they're exactly in sync with each other, but you can hardly get your timing right. You miss a step here, lose a beat there, and suddenly you stick out like a sore thumb.

This sense of "not fitting in" can be a powerful one and can often have a hefty impact on your self-esteem, especially when this hobby is one that you're enthusiastic about and really want to immerse yourself into. You can start to lose motivation and confidence over time and then you will eventually quit and never return to it again.

On the other hand, going out there and trying a new hobby can have a positive effect on your self-esteem if you remain positive about the whole experience. For example, maybe you can't get the beat right, but you've noticed that you're getting more fluid with the actual dance moves, and they're starting to come more naturally to you. Compare where you are now to where you began when you started, and you'd see that you're improving.

Realizing that you're getting better at something you love can boost your motivation to continue the hobby, increase your self-esteem, and make you feel more confident in your ability to learn new things. It can even carry on into new hobbies that introduce you to a whole new community of people who are ready to help you improve yourself one step at a time.

Your Position in Life

Where you are in life (may it be financially, emotionally, mentally, spiritually, or even physically) can have a large impact on your self-esteem. More specifically, how you *view* your position in life can change the way you're feeling and alter your self-confidence.

Take someone who is going through a really rough time. Maybe they have lost their job or house or been dealing with a rough divorce. They can either see it as the worst thing in the world or an opportunity to learn something new and start fresh. The path they decide to take will have a large impact on their self-esteem.

Imagine this person saying to themselves, "I lost my job, but that's okay because I know this is an opportunity to start somewhere new and fill in all the holes I had at my old job." It's easy to see how this positive view of the whole situation can bring about positive change inside the person. Now, imagine that same person saying, "I lost my job, which means I'll have no money, which means I'll have to sell everything to cover all of my debts. This is the worst thing in the world." Do you see how our perception of where we are in life can change the way we feel about ourselves?

Stuff like this happens all the time; that's just the way life is. However, how we react to these problems will often determine how we end up feeling about ourselves.

Significant Life Events

There are plenty of life events that can alter our self-esteem, for better or for worse. When a positive event happens, such as a kid's graduation, your wedding, or your 50th anniversary with the love of your life, we begin to feel more confident about ourselves. A kid's graduation tells us that we're good at raising children; a wedding tells us that we're lovable enough for someone to want to spend the rest of their lives with us; and the 50th anniversary tells us that we've been worth someone's love for the majority of your/their life.

Nevertheless, life events can also swing the other direction. When negative situations happen, such as a suicide in the family, a divorce with a loved one, or a child suddenly leaving the house and choosing not to talk to you, we begin to question our worth. Our confidence seems to dwindle as well. The suicide makes it appear like we didn't care enough for someone; the divorce tells us that we're not lovable; and the kid suddenly leaving home and cutting all ties with you implies that we failed as parents and ruined our kid's life. This is where blame starts to set in, and a vicious cycle of self-blame and self-hatred begins.

These life events aren't always avoidable, but they can help us understand why we are feeling a certain way and may push us to find ways to improve those feelings.

Remember, the first step to solving some of the issues in your life is identifying them.

Chapter 2
Self-Worth

Self-worth reflects our belief in the value we bring to the world. Self-worth, like self-acceptance, is not dependent on external circumstance.

Healthy self-worth is the basis of resilience in the face of adversity.

Here's a quick example to illustrate the benefits of having healthy self-worth.

A wealthy person who inherited most of their wealth could have high worth in society, yet they may consider themselves incredibly undeserving of it due to terrible self-worth. This may, in turn, keep them from trying to further the wealth they inherited.

To the contrary, a person who has become homeless due to a recent downfall may not be dismayed by the fact that they do not have a roof above their head because they view themselves as someone worthy of a residence.

In turn, this self-worth may keep them consistent in their approach to try and change their circumstances, regardless of how the world sees them.

Exercise: Self-worth improvement

This exercise is meant to help you see your value, even when we think you have little. If your answer to "Do you struggle with self-worth?" is "yes," this exercise is for you.

In your journal:

List all of what you believe you have done to help someone lead a better life. List as many as you can, but try to jot down at least twenty.

If you feel you have done nothing that deserves to be on that list, understand that this is not an aggregation of the most life-changing things you have done for others so far. Don't put yourself under pressure to come up with something significant.

Small gestures such as smiling back at someone or helping someone with the door, thanking the store clerk, or tipping more than usual, can all be included in this list. Random acts of kindness or whatever makes you feel good about making others happy, etc., also can make this list.

If you have been unusually low on the self-worth front, list 20 things daily until your self-worth starts to improve—until you start seeing the value you provide to others just by existing. Until you start to understand that *your existence matters*.

Ultimately, self-worth is about understanding that you are of value. Self-worth is also an understanding that you are fully capable of solving your problems.

Self-worth is strongly correlated to self-love. Developing self-love and self-acceptance builds your self-worth.

Chapter 3
The Importance of Being Self-Confidence

Self-confidence is a very important skill, and it gives you the ability to judge your own personal and social standing in accordance with your environment and also gain great satisfaction out of it.

There are many factors that influence self-confidence such as work environment, upbringing, as well as the drive or the level of commitment and enthusiasm towards pursuing a cause. Self-confidence is an essential element in developing and improving business ties as well as your personal life.

Just like the popular saying reminds us, as you begin the journey of your professional life, always have high confidence in the abilities you possess, because you have yet to prove your abilities.

This saying has been in circulation as far back as the evolution of the modern human society, yet the context couldn't be more accurate than it is today. More so than ever, in the present times that we live in, which are very competitive, self-confidence becomes a great asset, a source of strength, as well as self-sustenance for us.

But first, let's talk about self-confidence, why we need it, and how important it is in our lives.

Why Do We Need Confidence?

Knowing your strength and being confident about it can help you draw in courage and firm determination when things get difficult in life. Self-confidence helps provide perspective and gives you the courage to carry on when everyone else might view the road ahead or the task at hand to be almost impossible to carry out in the required time.

People who are confident have the ability to see and recognize what their limitations are and understand how to make up for their limitations with strength and resolve.

All that said, what you should understand is that self-confidence basically depends on your ability to handle actions, so let's talk briefly about the actions that can help in developing self-confidence.

Self-confidence Shows True Acceptance and Self-love

People with low self-confidence will mostly rely on the acknowledgment of others to make them feel important or get a sense of pride about themselves. Self-confident people don't need to get anybody's approval before they feel happy or proud of who they are. Self-confidence will help you realize or develop an attitude that no matter what challenges you face, or how difficult things get, you have promised yourself that you will always be there for yourself. It is like an unconditional acceptance of who you are.

Self-confidence and Positivism

Negativity or a negative mental attitude is toxic to both the physical and emotional well-being of the body. It can also affect the people around us and lead to us pushing them away. Nobody likes to hang around someone who always blames others for their own mistakes yet will never see their error, or ways to improve.

Self-confident people are typically optimists, because they are very confident in themselves, their skills, and their abilities, because they think positively and are not easily thrown off-track. They are confident about their course and are sure of succeeding, therefore they don't allow anything to hinder them nor worry about negativity.

Self-confidence Shows Maturity

When we pay too much attention and get too engrossed in the opinions of other people, we hinder our own path to happiness. When we start caring more about what we want and what we think and let our opinions and decision guide us, then we can enjoy life better in ways we planned to, or the way we want to live it.

One of the major signs of adolescent age is interest and expectations. According to the American Academy of Child and Adolescent Psychiatry (AACAP), adolescents usually appear sad, tearful, and mostly irritable, and there is a decrease in activities they used to be interested in. They become very sensitive to how people feel about or perceive them.

Self-confident people are usually more emotionally mature, and people who are emotionally mature are mentally healthy, make better rational decisions, are well attuned, and display a highly positive mental attitude towards themselves, their work, and other people around them.

Actions That Help Develop Self-Confidence

Self-confidence does better in an environment where you receive constructive feedback while the focus always remains on the positive.

As a confident person working in such an environment, you will be able to practice your skills and abilities far and above expectations. Meaning, you will be opportune to set goals, move beyond past mistakes, and learn new and exciting things.

Meanwhile, an environment where the expectations are impractical and you are always in comparison with others can gravely impede your self-confidence. When people are set as rivals to go against each other according to their performance in the game of numbers, self-confidence is harder to find.

Such circumstances can force you to develop or nurture a competitive mentality that is rather unhealthy. By making use of unjust and iniquitous means to achieve success, you could become ruthless in judging your self-performance, taking after unworthy people as role models and even underestimating or doubting your capabilities.

Such an atmosphere will create a workplace that is basically unhealthy due to the stress and pressure to outdo someone else's performance, instead of combining your energy as a team and work together while you help and assist each other to succeed. Some organizations actually do practice such method of pitting staff against each other and it works well. However, it peaks for a period of time, but most assuredly crashes.

High Self-Confidence

The approach people with high self-confidence employ to tackle problems is usually different from that of other people. They perceptually understand that building relationships is important and therefore, they have a knack for meeting new people, making new friends, and they get to share ideas and learn new things. This quality that they possess is one of the main reasons that they are so likable. Additionally, these highly self-confident people are always prepared to engage in conversations that highlight and grant mutual respect and equal importance to everyone that participated in it.

Another point about people who have high self-confidence is that they are fond of expressing what they think as well as their ideas in the presence of others.

This is because they are secure emotionally to the point that they can easily handle constructive criticism and rebuff the ones that are emotional. Meanwhile, that is not to say they are arrogant—quite the opposite, they are open and they present everyone with the opportunity to air their views.

Nonetheless, they are courageous enough to hold onto their decisions against all the antagonism to their ideas, especially when they believe and are convinced that they are doing the right thing or are on the right track.

Once you have made a decision and it is set in motion, there are two possible outcomes, which are that you have either made the right decision (success) or you made the wrong one (failure). But what distinguishes confident people from others is that when they succeed, they don't throw it in the faces of all those detractors.

Also, highly self-confident people are humble enough to admit to their mistakes and use that opportunity to learn from their failures. They have an objective mindset and approach with regards to both failure and success. That characteristic makes people with self-confidence respectable as well as lovable.

Low Self-Confidence

People who have low self-confidence have an awfully harsh and judgmental view of themselves, which when compared to the highly self-confident people means they are separated by a very wide gap. People with low self-confidence are susceptible to making emotional decisions instead of thinking rationally. They are more of the "let me stay in my corner" type in place of meeting new people, making new friends, and sharing new ideas. They avoid meeting new people or having company.

People with low-confidence are inclined to feel that they have nothing new, constructive, or consequential to contribute to any process. All these feelings combined with low self-worth and the total denial or avoidance to accepting changes make people with low self-confidence very prone to be undervalued and mistreated.

People with low self-confidence are mostly hesitant to share their views, thoughts, and opinions about things because they think they might be publicly mocked for their views. Naturally, it means their past interactions and experiences with others have little to no impact in enhancing their self-value and self-confidence in any way, therefore their views remain the same about their importance and productivity.

Everyone is bound to learn from their environment. The kind of people you meet and the type/quality of discussions you engage in with them directly affect and influence your self-confidence. On one hand, people who are very self-confident mix and interact with others and learn from those who they can learn from. On the other hand, low confident people believe they can't be who they are and that they will remain undervalued no matter what they try.

The Effects of Low Self-Confidence

People need role models who they can look up to and idolize as a compass to guide themselves and measure their own talents and skills, achievements, as well as compare their progress to in order to help them constantly improve themselves. That is exactly how people who are self-confident behave.

High self-confident people choose to interact with others and in that process, they share their views publicly in order to gain new perspectives, they keep improving on their skills, and they expand their knowledge constantly.

When people stop doing exactly that, what happens then? Well, without an anchor in their lives to hold them and stabilize them when they are drifting away, and without a model to tether on, they begin to lose focus. Without interaction with society, people will become extremely self-centered and only think about what concerns them, and it will be even more evident in how they take criticism. Everything will appear personal and even when constructive criticism is aired about their work, it will be assumed to be a personal attack.

The effect of low self-confidence will make people with such personalities think that they are less talented with inferior skills and abilities to handle and complete any assigned task. They feel unworthy to receive compliments and be appreciated. It gets even worse that when honest compliments are given for their efforts–it becomes a surprise or shock to them, hence they tag it as false, pretentious, or fake appreciation.

Chapter 4
When Self-Confidence Becomes Too Extreme

There are multiple ways in which a more extreme version of confidence that a person has with regards to him or herself can manifest. These include neglecting and not accepting particular circumstances and chances for continued growth and development due to the fact that a person has reached the conclusion that should he or she go forth and accept any of these circumstances that can could offer potential benefits to their well-being in the long-run, if they choose to accept them because they have been viewed as something that a person can do without any difficulty whatsoever. Moreover, these same people can reach the similar conclusion of developing the possible conviction that the person is supposedly so superior in their skillsets that he or she refuses to take on any new chance to hone their abilities because they believe that to do so would tarnish the embellished image that he or she has about themselves.

Such negative perceptive attitudes can even go in the opposite direction where a person believes that they have superhuman abilities which enables him or her to be able to juggle multiple opportunities, some of which do not fit the skills that they have mastered and due to their inability to refute these opportunities because they are aware that they cannot realistically complete any of these tasks since they lack the proficiency to perform such opportunities and tasks sufficiently. They find that their boatload of obligations increases dramatically as a consequence yet there is also the possibility that this embellished form of confidence that a person might display towards themselves can also cause the loved ones and other people who formulate the basis for their intimate social circle to distance themselves due to the fact that they do not appreciate the newly adopted conceited attitude that a person has been demonstrating as of late. People within the business organization that a person may be a part of can also adopt similar sentiments if they find that their co-worker is beginning to become too cocky with regards to their capabilities when in reality, there are certain capabilities that their co-worker actually lacks. Having too much confidence in oneself with regards to his or her abilities can also lead to an individual starting to neglect the worth and the abilities that his or her respective intimate partner within their shared relationship has or is trying to hone and develop further as he or she begins to concentrate most of their energy on exaggerating the amount of time that he or she spends with developing or flaunting his or her respective capabilities in the process.

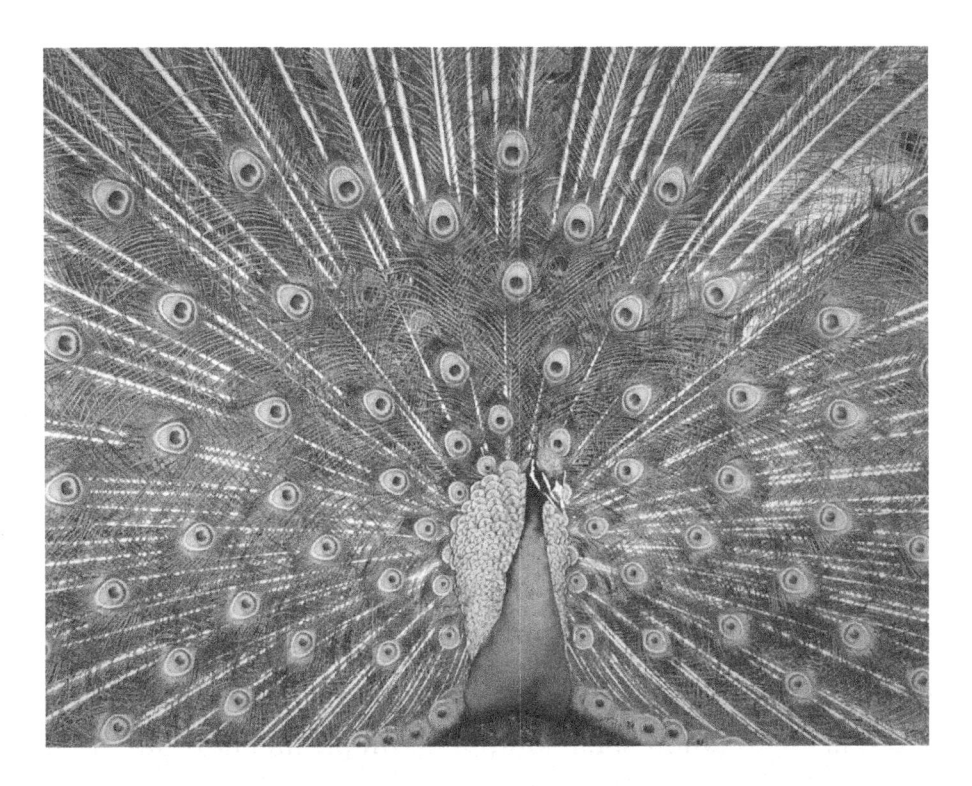

Research that conducted the possible negative effects that are correlated to a person who is found to display a large sense of confidence in their abilities and have a positive perception of themselves, has produced results which have indicated that young people in particular who were discovered to display a very strong sense of confidence in what they can do along with a highly elevated positive image of themselves had a higher chance of participating in activities where there was the chance that they would be placed in a predicament in which their well-being was put in jeopardy. It was also discovered that people with a heightened level of confidence in their abilities were more heightened to a point where it is considered to be too much were found to engage in intimate relationships that were toxic and unhealthy as these kinds of people have a behavioral pattern of deflecting the situations where their relationship indicates prominent issues solely onto the individual that he or she shares the romantic relationship with. People with these more extreme forms of convictions in their capabilities were also found to display tendencies that were linked to being more vicious and physically intimidating towards other people.

Of course, that is not to say that people cannot express any kind of confidence, there are plenty of positive manifestations that self-confidence can assume within a person. For on occasion, the people whose level of confidence in their own abilities that seems rather excessive can actually translate into a person being more likely to attain some kind of accomplishment or are used as mechanisms in order to deceive other people to come to the conclusion that they can, in fact, complete certain obligations when in fact the authentic skillsets that they have legitimately mastered do not realistically correlate with what they say they can actually do. Yet, there is the downside to displaying a heightened level of confidence which is linked to qualities that are expressed by a person within their respective personality which are linked to the disorder that is connected to being narcissistic or simply implying that a person is sneaky and unreliable, all of which are not admirable by people, especially by those who are part of the corporate world and are looking for new employees to fill the shoes of the positions that they are offering at the present.

Moderate cases where self-confidence can bubble up within specific people from time to time, for instance, cases where this can occur can include someone become unrealistic about meeting certain deadlines or not demonstrating the best effort that he or she can put forward when completing a designated task that has been assigned to him or her only to bear the grunt of the consequences that follow such choices. It is due to having to deal with such consequences that are negative in nature which enable such individuals who have found themselves in such negative circumstances to ponder whether these are choices that they want to make in the future and develop methods that they can put to effective usage in order to create more positive impressions on his or her co-workers and supervisors who are part of their full-time or part-time business organization. This is especially true if they have recently had to pay the price for submitting work that does not implement the highest form of quality that he or she can cultivate. However, in these particular scenarios, it is not so much a horrible state to briefly succumb to as long as people are able to learn from the errors that they have made and grow into more competent beings and professionals. Inevitably, to seek the oppositional course of action correlates strongly with the kinds of people who find that these tendencies have morphed into patterns of typical behavior which presents itself as all the more problematic and reflect a level of job performance and general attitude towards him or herself that is not practical and can cause their life to enter a downward spiral as a result.

At this point, you might be curious as to how a person can transmit the perceptions that he or she has with regards to their respective capabilities into an embellished form that causes their confidence with themselves to no longer be viewed in the same positive light that it might have been beforehand. There is not just a singular way that such potentially harmful transformations can take place as the methods that their own parental figures used in order to help formulate the kind of person that this respective individual shall become once he or she has reached the level of maturity in their life as well as the values and beliefs that make up the fabric of the cultural background that a person has been encouraged to adhere to and practice throughout their lifetime.

Moreover, key occurrences that caused such dramatic or minor changes to come to fruition within a person as they start to become more or less aware of the kind of being that they are emerging into and as their individual attitudes and perceptions begin to unfold. Within our own perspectives, what we desire, what is necessary, what we have gone through so far in life, what attitudes that we tend to exhibit towards ourselves, and what kind of cognitive processes tend to flow through the widest stretches of our brains are considered to hold a higher priority than what other people feel about themselves, what circumstances and events they go through, what other people need as well as what other people desire. There are other studies that elaborate further on the perceptions that people tend to exhibit towards themselves in the sense that due to the fact that people might think that they are superior or that they can complete certain tasks, this might lead them to embellish what they can actually do.

The way that they perceive themselves to be can lead to the consequence of forming their own ways of examining something that has nothing to do with them and turning it so that it mirrors solely what they have gone through in life and the convictions they display as well exclusively focusing on their own thoughts on the matter as opposed to also leaving room for considering the thoughts of other people. In short, it is better to have a view of your own worth that is a reflection of the kind of person that you truly are and not what you try to imitate in order to appear more confident overall.

Chapter 5
Guided Meditation Script - 20min

What is meditation?

Meditation, like hypnosis, is a method that can help change your state of consciousness. It is practiced in a wide variety of cultures, and often has spiritual overtones. But, while many religions involve meditation, it does not have to be a religious practice.

People meditate for a variety of reasons including stress reduction, increasing creativity, mental focus, and productivity, and for improving mental health as well.

Different types of meditation

Meditation is a big topic, and there are lots of different types. For example, concentration meditation involves thinking about nothing but a single object, word, or thought. In this type of meditation, if your mind wanders, as it will at first, you just gently direct it back to what you are meant to be thinking about. With practice, your mind will wander less, and your concentration will improve.

Mindful meditation involves allowing your mind to wander and examining your thoughts as they occur without judgment or malice. The intention is not to get involved with the thoughts or to judge them, but simply to be aware of each mental note as it arises.

Some kinds of meditation involve spending time cultivating feelings of peace, compassion, respect, and love. Others involve meditating as you move, thinking about your body, muscles, and breathing. Both yoga and tai chi are essentially forms of moving meditation.

Other forms of meditation involve trying to empty your mind of all thoughts and emotions but, needless to say, this is very hard !

In all forms of mediation, the aim is to take control of your mind and thoughts. This will help counteract many of the distracting and even unpleasant thoughts and sensations that normally reside within your mind.

The benefits of regular meditation

Studies reveal that regular meditation has a number of benefits including:

- Lowers an individual's blood pressure.
- Blood circulation is improved within the body.
- One experiences a lowered heart rate.
- The respiratory rate slows down.
- Anxiety lessens.
- Blood cortisol levels reduce (stress hormone).
- Well-being feelings become improved.
- Stress is reduced.
- There is deeper relaxation.

- One enjoys a wonderful sleep.

- An individual's creativity is heightened.

- Mental focus is improved.

- Energy levels in the body are improved.

- Happiness levels are improved.

- One gains more self-esteem and self-confidence.

How to meditate

If you have never tried meditation before, it's a good idea to start with an easy exercise to help you understand what meditation is and isn't. Once you feel happy with this basic introduction to meditation, you can try the guided meditation.

1. Sit or lie comfortably. The room should be warm but not hot, and quiet. You should not be disturbed.

2. Close your eyes.

3. Breathe slowly but naturally. Make no real effort to change how you breathe.

4. Focus your thoughts on your breathing. Note how your body moves each time you inhale and exhale. Feel the changes in your shoulders, chest, ribs, and abdomen as you breathe in and out.

5. Think only about your breathing. If any other thoughts or feelings enter your mind, acknowledge them but then gently refocus your mind on your breathing.

6. Continue for 3-5 minutes before returning to the present and getting on with your day.

7. Gradually increase the length of time you spend meditating as your ability to stay focused increases. However, don't force it – meditation in general should involve no mental effort.

Guided meditation script

Meditation can be self-guided which means you are responsible for the direction it takes. You choose what you are going to focus on and contemplate. Guided mediations involve meditating according to the input of an instructor – either in person or a pre-recorded script.

Guided meditations are useful, especially for beginners, because they give direction and structure to your meditation This is very useful if you find that your mind often wanders when you meditate alone.

Here is a script for a guided meditation. It is a general guided meditation script meant to help you relax and develop your meditation skill toolbox.

If you are driving or operating any sort of equipment that requires your attention, please do not go through this guided meditation session. Skip it and come back when you are fully available.

- Begin your meditation by becoming aware of your breathing. Breathe in through your nose, imagining your breath traveling down to your stomach. Feel your stomach swell as you breathe in.

- Hold your breath for a couple of seconds and then exhale through your mouth. Exhale slowly and completely but without forcing it.

- Continue to breathe slowly, in through your nose and out through your mouth. With each breath visualize your body become more relaxed.

- Bring your awareness to your feet. Take a breath in and exhale, taking any tension out of your feet. Your feet should feel warm, heavy, and relaxed.

- Focus on your breathing, ensuring it is slow and quiet, deep but not forced.

- Move your awareness to your lower legs. Take a breath in and then exhale, removing the tension from your calves and ankles. Your lower legs should feel warm, heavy, and relaxed.

- Focus on your breathing, ensuring it is slow and quiet, deep but not forced.

- Shift your focus to your thighs. Take a breath in and then exhale, removing the tension from your upper legs. Your thighs should feel warm, heavy, and relaxed.

- Focus on your breathing, ensuring it is slow and quiet, deep but not forced.

- Move your awareness to your hips. Take a breath in and then exhale, removing the tension from your hips and butt. Your hips should feel warm, heavy, and relaxed.

- Focus on your breathing, ensuring it is slow and quiet, deep but not forced.

- Shift your focus to your abdomen. Take a breath in and then exhale, removing the tension from your stomach. Your abdomen should feel warm and relaxed.

- Focus on your breathing, ensuring it is slow and quiet, deep but not forced.

- Move your focus to your heart. Breathe and imagine it opening like a beautiful flower. See your heart radiating a peaceful white light throughout your body.

- Focus on your breathing, ensuring it is slow and quiet, deep but not forced.

- Shift your awareness to your neck. Take a breath in and then exhale, removing the tension from your neck and throat. Your neck should feel warm, heavy, and relaxed.

- Focus on your breathing, ensuring it is slow and quiet, deep but not forced.

- Move your focus to your shoulders and arms. Take a breath in and then exhale, removing the tension from your upper body. Your arms and shoulders should feel warm, heavy, and relaxed.

- Focus on your breathing, ensuring it is slow and quiet, deep but not forced.

- Focus on your jaw and face. Take a breath in and then exhale, removing the tension from your head. Your jaw and face should feel warm, heavy, and relaxed.

- Focus on your breathing, ensuring it is slow and quiet, deep but not forced.

- Visualize a beam of healing green light entering the top of your head and traveling down your body, radiating outward and filling your torso and limbs. Allow this light to linger in the areas of your body that need healing. This could be a past physical injury, your broken heart, or just to quiet your mind.

- Expand this light to envelop your entire body, spreading healing power through every cell. Your whole body is now pulsing with healing energy as your heart beats and you breathe slowly and evenly.

- Your body is very relaxed now, and all your limbs feel warm, heavy, and relaxed. In fact, even if you wanted to move, you should feel like you can't. You are happy and comfortable where you are, and you may even want to smile.

- Now you are fully relaxed, return your internal gaze to your heart. Picture it as an open flower, full of love and vitality. Imagine it growing and blooming outward toward the power and warmth of the sun. Your heart is full of boundless love for yourself and those around you. In return, the people you meet love and respect you too.

- Hold your focus on your heart for a moment. If uninvited thoughts enter your mind, just gently push them away and shift your focus back to your heart.

- As you breathe, repeat these mantras silent to yourself:

- I am happy and I am relaxed

- I am filled with joy and love

- I find it easy to smile and do so often

- Happiness comes easily to me

- There is joy in everything I do

- Rest and breathe for a moment, bathing in the warmth of your happiness and relaxation. Enjoy this feeling and notice how calm and content you feel.

- When you are ready, bring your awareness back to the room you are in. Gently wiggle your fingers and toes. Make small circles with your wrists and ankles. Gently flex your elbows and knees. Open your eyes and return to this moment in time and space.

Chapter summary

Meditation is a powerful tool that helps you learn to control your thoughts and emotions. There are lots of different types of meditation, and some of them are very spiritual. Regardless of your religious beliefs, meditation can help you reduce stress, increase mental focus, lower your blood pressure, and increase creativity.

Meditation can be as simple as sitting quietly and thinking about your breathing or involve various mental tasks, as in a guided meditation. Meditation can take time to learn, but it is very rewarding and can improve many aspects of your mental and physical wellbeing.

Chapter 6
How to Visualize Success and Bring It to Life

Visualization can be best described as seeing yourself where you want to be or belong when you have attained your life goals and missions. This chapter provides you with step by step strategies that you can use in life to ensure that you are making the right decision towards the achievement of your personal life goals. In visualization, the more you see many positive things the more you advance in your life goals and the more you advance in your life goals the more opportunities come into your life.

Most winners, actually almost all winners and highly successful people, use the art of visualization in life. Some use this technique knowingly while others find themselves visualizing without clearly noting that they are actually visualizing. You always have to make your imaginative mind work for you to put things, which are in your plans, into fruition. The only limit to success is always your mind and thus, if you think positively, and see your goals into reality with your mind, you automatically unleash the guts to work into your life missions and goals with the sense that you will actually achieve them. You gain certainty and power.

Goals Visualization

The first step in the visualization process is visualizing the activity, results or events that you desire to achieve. Thoughts become things. In this case you get what you think. Creativity and synthesis of the mind will take the lead of what you desire to get in life. You should consider closing your eyes and then figuring out the picture you have after you have achieved your goals, after you are successful or during an event when you are successful.

For example, if you want to be promoted from your current position at work, you can start by picturing yourself in a new office. Picture yourself doing something new in the office. You can also picture yourself on a new chair, or new desk with a new tag. By doing this, you make the big stuff, namely the promotion, seem smaller.

Fixing Your Mind-Set During the Visualization Process

You will never improve nor achieve anything when you have the feeling of being miserable in your life. A negative mindset leads to negative achievements, while, positive mindsets lead to positive achievements in life, always be optimistic, be positive and view things in the positive perspective. Always focus on success and success will follow you. You can never visualize failure and expect to achieve anything in life. An effective visualization process is depicted by positive thoughts. Make your goals and desires part of your life.

Moving Your Imagination into the Real World

Spending all your time; moments, days, months and even years visualizing without working will only make you to stagnate on one rank or level in life. You've got to move into the real world. This implies that, even after you have undergone the visualization process, you have to work. Working ensures that you have put what you are actually visualizing into reality. You should start by focusing on you being there, and you have achieved the goal or success that you want, focus (plan) on how you will achieve it in the real life and then work on it, knowing that you will actually achieve it.

For example, picture a soccer player who wants to hit a ball. The first thing is always placing the ball on the right place on the ground, and then moving back some few steps, figuring out the picture of him hitting the ball, that is stroke after stroke or even one stroke, and then actually hitting the ball. That is how all other things are achieved in the real world.

Always Remind Yourself of the Significance of Slowing Down

You can only visualize when you are at ease, calm and focused. Thus, when using this technique, always calm down, be at peace; both physical peace and peace of mind. Always be sure that you have freed yourself from any worries. Just like meditation, ensure that your mind is focused and peaceful. This will ensure that the act is done vividly and actively. There is no rush! Just relax and stay calm!

Have a Visualization of your Personality Traits

For example, if you are visualizing yourself being the president, you will want to visualize yourself in the presidency. You will want to see yourself in the White House and on the Presidential seat. You will want to visualize yourself delivering presidential speeches. But this is not all! You also need to visualize some of the key personal traits that will give you the qualities of a president. You have to visualize things like: respect, discussion, ability to deflect criticism, sharing, listening, smiling, persuasiveness as well as communication.

It is also advisable to have a visualization of your career in life. Things and traits which affect your career, your mission in life, your core values as well as the tagline that you will be using for you to actually do what is right to achieve your goals.

Using Affirmations

Just like pictures, in the visualization process words work great too. After you have achieved the "smaller bits" of your life goals, always say loudly 'I have done this and this and I am going there'. This gives you courage to progress.

Refining your Visualization Techniques

Never think of changes overnight, this is just like thinking of being disappointed on the next day. Always have some long-term dreams. Have hopes, dreams, goals, and successes that are figured out like, 3, 5, or even 10 years in the future. This is where you can start your visualization process. You can, as well, write down some of the outcomes that you want after this time. In the visualization process always think deeper.

You should also ensure that you are always realistic with your goals both in the visualization process and in the real world. Don't imagine yourself as another person, but visualize yourself as you after you have achieved your goals. By visualization you perfectly achieve more, as your mind is the only obstacle to your success!

Chapter 7
Self-Acceptance Habits That Lead to Improved Wellbeing

Self-acceptance is about being aware of your strengths and weaknesses, having a subjective view of your capabilities, worth, skills, talents and feeling satisfied with the person you are at present despite your weaknesses, deficiencies, past mistakes, or endeavor to better yourself. When you accept yourself as you are, you practice self-understanding and self-love and because of it, your mental health and sense of self-worth improves.

The best way to practice self-acceptance and therefore improve your wellbeing, self-esteem, and self-growth (and therefore success and peace) is to practice self-love.

The following habits and practices will help you with that aim:

1: Practice Daily Self-Care

We spend a large portion of our daily lives fulfilling our obligations to our jobs, partners, spouses, kids, community, etc. Because of this, many of us fail to dedicate time to ourselves, which is understandable because when your life is busy, carving out time to do something you love seems like a waste. It's not!

2: Stop Comparing Yourself to Others

When you implement this habit, you will notice an immediate improvement in your sense of self (self-worth and self-esteem).

We spend a large portion of our lives comparing our personalities, lives, and achievement to those of our immediate and social friends. When you compare yourself to someone else—especially when you compare your achievements to that of a friend or acquaintance—you are essentially denying your individuality: *that you are unique and therefore have unique aims, talents, weaknesses, strengths, etc.* Because of this 'comparison disease,' many of us spend a large portion of our day thinking we are "less than and competing in a race we cannot win because no one can be better at 'you' better than you."

The next time you notice yourself comparing your achievements to those of a social media friend, remind yourself that the only person you should be competing against is the person you were yesterday.

3: Mind Your Self-Talk

Low self-esteem is a by-product of constantly berating and beating yourself, which is in itself a by-product of negative self-talk.

For instance, if you often think, "no matter what I try or how hard I work, I cannot seem to achieve success with women," question the authenticity of this thought by looking for evidence for and against it. Then, replace it with a positive and compassionate thought such as, "the more I experiment with various strategies, the closer I get to personal success with women, dating, and relationships."

When you do this daily—or as often as you can, which becomes easier when you practice conscious intentionality—your inner voice changes to a positive one that fosters a sense of peace, self-esteem, wellbeing, and personal success and satisfaction with the direction in which you are steering your life.

4: Get Enough Sleep

Sleep is a basic human need, and one of our most overlooked self-love habits. Thanks to our busy lives, we rarely get enough sleep, which is such a shame because sleep deficiency is a catalyst for ailments such as chronic stress and anxiety (and depression), heart disease, diabetes, and many others including a constant sense of lethargy (being low of energy), and demotivation in your day-to-day life.

Getting 7-10 hours of sleep every day is not an act of selfishness. It's an act of self-love that increases your wellbeing, feelings of peace, and because being well-rested improves your energy, getting enough sleep also means improved energy and productivity, which means increased ability to take action that increase your chances of success, and as you know, feeling you're working towards achieving something increases your self-worth.

5: Practice Daily Journaling

Writing is one of the most cathartic exercises in existence.

When you make journaling a daily part of your life by journaling every morning, evening, and every chance you get, you get painful or negative thoughts on paper and therefore off your mind where had you allowed them to ferment, would have had a negative influence on your spirit/psyche.

The introspection that comes with the practice of daily journaling also helps you become more aware of your needs, strengths, weaknesses, aims, advantages, etc. This improves your sense of self, and according to Alison Ledgerwood, a professor at the University of California, it boosts your sense of gratitude as well as your sense of physical health.

6: Practice Relaxed Awareness

Relaxed awareness is very similar to mindfulness and conscious intentionality. The main difference between these practices is that with relaxed awareness, the aim is to practice present consciousness and acceptance of whatever is as it is right now.

For instance, the practice asks you to become aware of your judgments, self-criticism, thoughts, pains, weaknesses, etc. and to accept them nonjudgmentally without needing to judge yourself or needing to embark on implementing any form of change.

Relaxed awareness is essentially the ability to become aware of your existence as it is without wanting to change whatever is occurring in the moment. When practiced consistently, relaxed awareness makes you aware of your body, mind, thoughts, and feelings, and their ever-changing nature.

To practice it, take a moment to close your eyes and rather than focus on your breath, become aware of everything that is in the present moment: your thoughts, feelings, etc. Just watch your consciousness and every guarantee is that your sense of personal wellbeing shall elevate.

7: Free Yourself from the "Should" Mentality

A majority of us spend a large portion of our lives chained to the concept of should: *"I should be this or that, I should do this or that, I should have achieved this or that by now, I should feel X or Y,"* etc.

Marrying yourself to this mentality is playing into the comparison game, which is detrimental to your self-esteem, self-confidence, peace of mind, self-worth, and chances of success.

To pull yourself by the bootstraps, embark on the journey to self-growth, and free yourself from the "should" mindset, practice moment-to-moment mindfulness and conscious intentionality. These practices help make you aware of instances when you tend to use the phrase, "I should be----____."

Out of this awareness, you can then reconnect with your intention: what you are doing and why you are doing it. Where your intention does not align with your aims or what you want to accomplish, you can make a shift that turns the occurring negative inner chatter into a positive inner chatter that is conducive to personal growth and an enhanced sense of self-worth, peace, and personal achievement.

8: Practice Daily Realism

The kind of realism we are talking about here is being realistic with your capabilities but especially about what you can and cannot achieve within a specified period.

Low self-esteem often breeds out of feeling inadequate, which is in itself a by-product of biting off more than you can chew or expecting too much from yourself and others—and feeling disappointed and defeated when things fail to pan out as planned.

Having goals is an amazing way to live purposefully, but whenever you set out to achieve certain goals or aims, always ask yourself, *"Am I being realistic about what I can comfortably achieve within this given time?"* If not, realign your time and priorities so that you have more time to do the things that infuse your daily life with joy and positive energy, the very things that lead to self-esteem, self-actualization, and personal success.

Chapter 8
Exercises to Set and Achieve Goals

Think about all of the ways that you have begun to think about tackling self-confidence issues at this point. So many of them require you to do something actionable, but how do you actually get moving on those things? Sure you can try to break things down, but how do you really begin to think about what you need to do in the first place?

When you are faced with not knowing what to do or what is going on, one of the best possible ways you can start to tackle things is simply through learning to utilize goals. Goals themselves may be something that you have never bothered with—after all, most goals go completely unfulfilled, so what is the point, right?

That is the same self-defeating behaviors that cause so many other problems as well and that sort of thinking needs to be abandoned immediately. When you reject that thinking altogether, you can begin to use goals the way they are truly intended to be—through making sure that you can actually see things through to the end, you will be able to not only meet your goals but also ensure that you are able to boost your self-confidence.

Goals and Self-Confidence

Goals are effective plans that will allow you to do something that you need to do. When you are able to set a goal, you are able to plan out what you are doing, the steps to success, and, ideally, how to know when you are done with the goal in the first place. When you have a goal written out for yourself, you can begin to work toward something.

Working toward something is the perfect way to ensure that you build self-confidence. However, self-confidence is largely linked to whether you succeed or not. When you have good motivation, you are able to recognize that you are doing what you wanted or needed to get done. This can help you with your self-confidence simply because you will be actively doing something. Succeeding toward that goal and having something that you strive for implies that you trust yourself to actually succeed in doing so. That is effectively utilizing your self-confidence to make sure that you are doing what is necessary to actually achieve the goal.

Of course, if you fail to meet your goal, you will likely feel quite disappointed in yourself. You will probably feel like this is a recurring pattern and that you always fail your goals, so why bother trying in the first place? Your self-confidence suffers because you have failed yet again and you do not know what to do that will make things better.

While your goals will directly impact your self-confidence, it is important that you will be setting goals that you can actually achieve. When you do so, you will make sure that you are setting goals that are not just setting yourself up for failure, which would be problematic to your self-confidence. By setting yourself up for failure, you will effectively make it impossible for yourself to do anything other than ruin your self-confidence further.

How to Achieve Life Goals Through Self-Esteem and Self-Confidence

In this section, we will look at the ways in which your self-esteem and self-confidence can impact your ability to achieve your life goals.

When you have a high level of self-esteem, you are able to approach pitfalls and moments of discouragement with resilience. You are able to bounce back from negative outcomes because you have the belief that you tried your best and that this was a one-time downfall. You are able to fully believe that you will still achieve positive results the next time you try. Being able to be resilient is extremely important when it comes to achieving goals. Without a doubt, everyone will face setbacks and times when things become difficult, and being able to push through these times without becoming discouraged is essential to reaching those big life goals you set for yourself. You see yourself as a capable human being and someone who is just as deserving as anyone else, which makes you more successful than someone who cannot see themselves this way.

If someone has low self-esteem, they likely cannot see why they are deserving of achieving their goals, and this may make them feel discouraged. These feelings of discouragement can hinder their performance in things that would be steps on the way to achieving their goals. These people may decide to quit because they feel that the process is too hard and that they aren't cut out for it. They may feel as though they don't have the resources to reach the goals they have set for themselves or may even refrain from setting goals in the first place for fear of failing at achieving them.

For someone who has a high level of self-confidence, they are likely comfortable seeking help and support from anywhere they can get it when it comes to achieving their goals. This could be in the form of sports psychologists who would help with their mental performance, or physiotherapists to keep their body in good shape if this was a sports-related goal. These people feel that there is no shame in asking for help or using all of the resources available to them, as they shamelessly ask for what they need in order to further themselves on the journey to their goals.

These people are likely also much more comfortable sharing their goals and dreams with people in conversation, which motivates them and also tells everyone else that this person is open to receiving anything they can give in the form of support, even if it is an encouragement. By having more people know about the goals you are working towards, it not only tells them that they could help you, but it keeps you motivated and accountable to this goal because more people know about it than just you.

This does not mean that a person with low self-esteem or low self-confidence is less competent and less able to achieve their goals, but the fact that they would tend to keep quiet about their goals and refrain from asking for help on their way to achieving their goals makes it harder for them to succeed. If nobody other than the person themselves knows about the goals, they are trying to reach. It makes it easier for them to back out of it or give up on it. There is nobody else holding them accountable for these goals, which can cause them to feel like they have no support.

Without asking for help, they are not doing everything they can to achieve their goals. If it is music-related goals, for example, the person may benefit from extra lessons, talking to a professional musician, or going to their local music shop to get information about the best new instruments. If they do not have the self-confidence to believe that they are able to come close to achieving their goals, they may be foregoing all of these things that would help them to get there, which means that they are causing themselves a self-fulfilling prophecy by standing in the way of their own success.

A person with low self-confidence may also spend time beating themselves up after a performance that doesn't go as well as they would have liked, which demotivates them and also takes up time that they could spend practicing if they had been able to bounce back quicker.

Setting vs. Achieving Goals

Keep in mind that there is a massive difference between setting your goal and achieving your goal, and for that reason, you need to make sure that you are setting goals in a format that is actually something you can handle. You want to make sure that you form goals that are effectively achievable so you do not just bomb your self-confidence for no good reason. The best way to do this is to follow the guide that will be provided below for SMART goals. When you set goals the SMART way, you can ensure that you are setting goals that are meaningful and achievable for you while also making sure that you did not set a goal that was so simple, you would achieve it with no effort.

After all, how satisfying would it be to sing your ABCs as an adult? Most likely, it would not be satisfying at all, but to a 3-year-old, singing that song may be the best thing he has done all week. The 3-year-old deserves to be proud of himself for doing so, though an adult proud of singing the ABCs might get some strange looks from those around him or her. Adults should know their ABCs already, whereas preschoolers tend to be learning it.

Bad Goals

Before we begin to understand what goes into a good goal, we must first identify what does not go into a goal. If you set a bad goal, you run the increased risk of that goal being entirely unattainable, and an unattainable goal is a goal destined for failure no matter how hard you may try to succeed. Ultimately, when you are setting a goal, there are three criteria that you want to avoid as much as possible: You want your goal to avoid being rooted in an emotional state, rooted in the past, or are rooted in negativity rather than being something positive.

When you set a goal that falls for one of those three problems, you are likely going to see that goal fail, and that is going to do no favors for that self-confidence that you are trying to bolster up.

When you make a goal that is rooted in an emotional state, you are telling yourself something like, "I want to be happy," which may seem like a good goal at first glance, but stop and consider for a moment what emotions are. Your emotions are nothing but fickle, fleeting states of mind that come and go incredibly quickly. They are there to help you respond to your environment, and for the most part, how you feel is going to happen whether you want to or not. While you can control your reaction to your emotions, it is incredibly difficult to prevent your emotions from playing out; however, they are inclined to play out. When you turn your attention toward being happy, all you are saying is that you will only be successful in the small amount of time that you are happy, and that time will be fleeting. No one is happy all the time.

When you make a goal rooted in the past, all you are doing is refusing to acknowledge that you are currently in the present. Instead of seeing the past as something that has happened and can be learned from, you are instead saying that you wish to return to the past altogether. You are trying to reject who you are now, and even if your goal is well-intentioned, such as saying that you want to be the person you were in college, meaning that you want to lose some weight and be more outgoing, you are rejecting the person that you are now. That is problematic as well as that means that you are unhappy with who you are, and you are still setting yourself up for failure because you can never go back to the past, despite your best wishes to do so.

When you set your goal as something negative or avoidant, such as, "I don't want to feel sad anymore," you are doing two things wrong—first you are setting your goal to be dependent upon an emotion, and you are also setting your goal to be negative. Your goal is worded in a negative fashion that means that you are thinking in a negative fashion. When your mindset controls everything, you want to make sure that your mindset is a positive one to ensure that you are not falling for any other negative behaviors in your life. You cannot possibly choose to avoid and reject all negative thoughts unless they are your goals—that is still keeping your mind rooted in negativity.

Setting SMART Goals

When you want to set a goal, what you should do is try to set your goals in a SMART manner. SMART stands for specific, measurable, achievable, relevant, and timed. When you make sure that your goal checks off all of those boxes, you know that your goal will be well-formed and actionable, meaning that it will help you make sure that you can achieve it. This may seem intimidating at first, but you can make use of this process quite simply.

Specific

When your goal is specific, you are making sure you have narrowed your goal down as much as you possibly could. You make sure that you are actively doing something that will be beneficial to yourself by knowing exactly what you will do. The more specific, the easier it is to know exactly where you are aiming. For example, consider the difference between saying your goal is to move to Colorado and saying that you will move to Boulder, Colorado. When you say that you will move to Colorado, there are many different places that you could mean, and it is not particularly clear where you mean. However, specifying it down to a city, or even a neighborhood, can help you immensely.

When you are setting your goal, make sure that you are always embracing the most specific goal that you can. If you want to lose weight, specify how much. If you want to get into running, specify how much you want to be able to run on a regular basis.

If you want to learn something new, specify what it is that you wish to learn—do you want to learn a new language? A dance? A song? A hobby? The options are limitless, and when you limit your goal down and specify one thing, you make it easier to work with.

Measurable

Next, you must make sure that you can measure your goal in some way. You may measure it through a certain quantity, such as losing weight or a 10-minute mile. You may also measure it through percentages or instances; for example, saying that you smoke and want to cut down is not particularly specific. However, saying that you smoke 10 cigarettes a day and want to cut down 7 of them is, and it is measurable.

If your goal is trying to cut down on outbursts of some kind, such as wanting to eliminate panic attacks, there are still options for you to use. You can choose to cut down by the number of average panic attacks you feel in a week. If you feel like you suffer from a panic attack at least 10 times a week, for example, you could say that you want to cut that down 70% over a month-long period. That means that you would want to cut out 7 of those panic attacks.

There are always ways that you can figure out how to make your goal measurable in some capacity—the trick is figuring out how to do so.

Achievable

At this point, you need to make sure that your goal is something that you can truly do. You want to analyze whether it is something that is doable, and if it is doable, you need to break down your plan and begin to work toward it. Write down or plan out all of the steps that you would need to meet in order to be sure that you were, in fact, able to achieve your goal.

Relevant

Sometimes, just knowing whether you can do something is not enough to determine whether it is actually relevant to you. When you want to figure out if it is relevant, you are wondering if what you have set as your goal is something that you can, in fact, do, and if you can do it, you are asking if it is meaningful or something that you *would* do. Think about this for a moment—how meaningful would it be for a marathon runner to decide that he wants to run a mile as his goal? There is already a good chance that he has the stamina to run a mile if he can run literal marathons—so why would he set this goal? When you make sure that your goal is relevant, you are ensuring that it actually makes sense as a goal and that you actually want or need to achieve it.

Timed

This step is quite simple—you are simply setting yourself up with a deadline for your goal. You are saying that your goal will end at one specific point in time and that if you have not achieved it by that point, then you have failed and that is the end. You need to have an ending point for your goal if you truly want to be successful at setting one. Without the ending point, it becomes incredibly easy to simply push off your goal over and over again. You could simply keep telling yourself that you are going to achieve your goal tomorrow... Over and over again. Eventually, you never actually do it and there needs to be a point at which you simply call it and say that the goal is failed. There is no shame in failing, but you need to acknowledge that you have failed if it has been three months and you have made no progress at all.

Holding Yourself Accountable

Another method of making sure that you can actually achieve your goal is to find a way to makes yourself accountable. Perhaps the best way to do this is to announce your intention to achieve one specific goal and document it as you go for people on, for example, social media. Perhaps you want to lose 30 lbs by Christmas and you decide that you will broadcast it within a group dedicated to people trying to achieve their goals. You can then post up your progress as you achieve more and more. As you do this, you effectively make it so other people are aware of your goal, and you will feel more driven to achieve it when you have people acting and expecting it.

This works for several different types of goals—you simply set up a way to hold yourself accountable and you make sure that you then follow through with it. Your method of holding yourself accountable should keep you driven or motivated. After all, if you have friends or family that will stop to ask you how the diet and exercise is going, you are more likely to continue. You do not want to have to tell your friend or family member that you have failed or that you gave up on your goal because you were not making the necessary progress, so you work harder out of obligation.

Finding an Accountability Buddy

Even better, you can take your accountability a step further. In finding an accountability buddy, you are finding someone that you can use to keep you accountable because you are both working toward the same goal. If your goal is to lose those 30 pounds, then match up with someone else that wants to lose 30 pounds too. If you do so, you can both work together toward the process.

You may both decide to diet and exercise, as by and large, that is the most normal course of action when you want to lose weight. In deciding your diet and exercise routine, you both agree to similar terms and agree to similar cheat days or opportunities. When you do this, you effectively allow yourself to have a plan to work toward that you are working on with someone else. While it may still seem intimidating to you, you will find that progress is easier when you have someone with you along the way.

Not only will it seem like less work when you have a friend with you, you will also want to make sure that you are not letting your friend down. If you do not go to the gym as agreed, you are forcing your friend to go alone or not at all, and that means that you are putting your friend in a bad spot as well. That keeps you driven to work toward your goal further simply because you do not want to let down your accountability buddy.

Chapter 9
How to Develop Charisma

There are many components to improving your social skills. One of the best things you can do to improve your social skills drastically is working towards building your charisma. Charisma is that magnet that you need to draw people to you, enter a room and take charge without feeling cocky and make others believe in you and your idea. It is a vital part of the characteristic that every leader must have to win the utmost devotion of their followers.

Some people are lucky to be born with charisma, while others learn to cultivate it. However, the good news is that you can take a creative step to develop charisma. In my research, charisma consists of a set of traits that can be divided into behaviors that anyone can imbibe.

For the purpose of this book, we will be exploring the three categories of charisma. In other words, we will be exploring how you can develop charisma under the umbrella categories: presence, power, and warmth.

How to Develop Charisma: Presence

We have all been involved in the conversation when we can tell that the other person is not fully present. This is not surprising as there are many things that serve as a distraction. With the invention of smartphones and social media, it seems that people now have to alternate between two worlds. In a bus ride or a train ride, I am pretty sure half of the passengers will have their attention buried in their mobile device.

My idea is not to paint these developments as bad. However, my point is to see why this is affecting your full engagement with people and how you can set yourself aside.

Being charismatic is much different than making people think of you as an interesting and awesome person. I am not interested in teaching you tricks to blow your trumpets. The secret is in developing tricks to make people feel important such that they are left feeling so much better after their meeting with you, they look forward to more!

As social beings, we all love the attention and crave acknowledgment. This is partly one of the main reasons we make friends, fall in love, and do things to impress each other and seek validation from others. The good news is that it is rather simply to make people feel good and wanted. If you are shy or socially awkward person, it will be easy for you.

Conveying presence is pretty simple yet could be difficult for a large number of people. You have to determine and be intentional about directing your attention to someone. The good news is, you can, with practice, develop and imbibe this skill.

How can you develop a presence? Here are some tips that can be of tremendous help:

Be Sure You are Physically Comfortable

Attention will be pretty difficult if all that occupies your thoughts is how tight your pair of shoes is. We will discuss the part of dressing in developing charisma. This calls for being comfortable in your skin such that you have nothing demanding your attention.

Besides, it will also be difficult to concentrate if you are uncomfortable due to a headache or physical pain in any part of your body. This calls for consciously taking care of yourself. Be sure you sleep well and do not overcome yourself.

Have Your Mobile Device Out of Sight

In addition to having your mobile device out of sight, you also need to silence them. This removes the distraction that any notification might cause. And when it is out of sight, your friend gets the notion that you are completely invested in the conversation. It is a good way to show respect as well since checking your mobile at the sound of every notification obviously signifies your distraction.

Try and Maintain Eye Contact

Looking others in the eye carries a lot of meaning. On the surface, however, it signifies honesty, interest warmth, competence, and mental stability. It also shows that you are interested in and invested in the conversation, as opposed to looking elsewhere. With eye contact, you also get to improve the quality of your conversation and create a sense of connection that brings live and warmth into the conversation.

It is, however, important not to give someone a cold stare as it could be intimidating and plain uncomfortable. It is okay to look elsewhere once a while, but not so much as to get distracted with other things. Your attention should be on the person you are talking; hence, your eyes and other parts of your body should be directed at the person.

Let Your Nod Signify You Are Listening

In addition to maintaining eye contact while having a conversation, it is important to give nodding gestures to let the other person know you are listening. This is not about nodding to every statement as it might send the wrong message. You want to make sure you listen to the person, you understand, and you agree with your nods. Bear in mind that excessive nodding can seem like desperation to please and agree with the person, and this, you do not want.

Be Comfortable with Some Seconds of Silence

In other words, do not feel pressured to start blabbing when the other person finishes talking. Many people are guilty of this, and it takes patience and practice to develop this character. While the other person is talking, grant the person the courtesy of your attention and do not be pressured to rack your brain on the response you will give. Doing this will divide your attention, robbing you of the opportunity to fully grasp the message being passed across. When the person is done talking, wait for a couple of seconds before responding.

How to Develop Charisma: Power

When we talk about power in relation to charisma, it is not about the ability to command people or be the president or leader of a group. Real power, charismatic power is found in the humblest walks of life. It is the ability to affect people and the world around.

Charismatic power, in this sense, is more about how people perceive you. It is not about having a million dollars in your account or knowing some powerful people. It is neither about having the ability to command people nor having a battalion of soldiers at your disposal. When we talk about charismatic power, the following point explains how to develop it:

Increase Your Knowledge in Many Things

Besides your area of expertise, having a little knowledge of many things is a good idea. For someone to be able to affect and influence the world around, he must be intelligent. The idea behind this is to be able to fit into any conversation with ease. The best ways to accomplish this is by reading and watching documentaries. Embrace every avenue to gain knowledge. With this, people will see you as confident and charismatic.

Dress for Power

What is the first thing that comes to your mind when you see people dressed in military uniform? We automatically think they command power and authority. The point here is not to dress like the navy seal or a detective to command power and respect from others. To influence people positively, you need to be mindful of your dressing. Bear in mind that your clothing is part of the few things that helps people form their first impression about you.

Even besides commanding respect, dressing well has a way of making you feel confident about yourself. It is important I point out here that dressing well is not about getting the latest designer clothes to look powerful. Make sure your clothing is neat and well pressed. Get rid of worn out and torn clothing. You can also have your clothes tailored so they look better and fitted on you. Use a blazer or coat to broaden, and highlight your shoulder, invest in a pair of shoes to look smart.

Get Comfortable Taking up Space

In the animal kingdom, alpha males like agama lizard, dogs, wolves, lions etc., mark off spots with their urine, feces, and their scents to demarcate their territory. These alpha males defend their territory fiercely, and other animals will keep away to prevent confrontation. The idea behind this example is that taking up space is also a way to appear powerful. This is also one of the attributes of powerful people. The idea is not about resorting to animalistic behaviors to take up space.

Rather, the idea is about using subtle ways to increase the space you occupy. When a friend comes to chat, sit on the table with a side butt or put your arm around the back of a chair. When you go out for a drink, be comfortable having your wallet, car keys and mobile phone on the table.

Get Comfortable with Power Poses

Have you ever wondered why superheroes in comic books are usually illustrated with their hands akimbo? It is because having the hands akimbo communicates power. There are quite a number of poses you can assume to convey power. In a meeting, for instance, if you are to talk, you can rest your hands on the desk and lean forward slightly.

The interesting part about these power poses is that besides making others see you as powerful, it also has a way of making you feel powerful. Thus, to increase your confidence level, be sure to try incorporating power poses for a few minutes. With your confidence level boosted, you can act powerful, which helps build your charisma.

Speak Slowly and Speak Less

It is not all about taking up physical space to be powerful. You need to get comfortable dominating your conversation, with silence. Bear in mind, however, that this differs from greedily hoarding the conversation period. Rather, it is being comfortable with speaking slowly. Bear in mind that the lesser your words, the more value they carry. This is one powerful secret a few people know. This is why skilled interrogators use silence and fewer words to make suspects uncomfortable. This causes the suspect to babble on, in the desperation of filling up space, which eventually rats him out.

Awkward silence is not an issue for this set of people, and rather they revel in it. Even when not in an interrogation setting, the other man anxiously and unconsciously gives out sensitive information in a bid to fill the awkward silence.

It is not about taking up space in conversation alone. You need to get comfortable speaking slowly as well. You do not want to appear nervous. With slow speaking, however, you convey calmness and intelligence, the attributes of powerful people.

Work on Your Composure

In other words, boost your poise. Carry yourself with dignity and grace. Even if you are nervous, hide it and do not make it obvious. In addition to that, pick your words carefully without relying excessively on verbal fillers. Then act naturally and be still, without nodding excessively at every statement made. Do not fidget excessively.

In conclusion, acting powerful is way different from being a jackass. In other words, for you to be truly charismatic, the power you developed need to work in sync with other elements of developing charisma. It is also important to note that being charismatic is not the same as being nice. While being nice is good, you will not come off as magnetic with the ability to command and draw people. This is why working on developing charisma will be of terrific help.

How to Develop Charisma: Warmth

The final piece of the puzzle in developing charisma is warmth. Warmth is your ability to be seen as caring, approachable, and making people feel at ease. Right from a tender age, all humans are wired to crave attention. It is a need that is rooted deeply in all humans. This is why we seek love in the first place. Warmth is the desire for a hug after seeing our loved ones for a while. It is the desire for a hot cup of beverage on a winter morning. It is that desire for attention from our parents when we do well on our test.

Even though we all grow with time, deep down, there will always be a part of us that craves for warmth. It is important to note that you need to genuinely possess this character genuinely. Warmth, unlike other elements of charisma, cannot be faked. It is easy to pretend to be genuinely interested in what people have to say, and you can easily fake power by assuming power poses and taking up space. But faking warmth is not that easy because people oftentimes can tell if you are nice to them in a bid to get something from them.

Your warmth can come off as sincere. However, it needs to be rooted in something deep, other than a selfish motive. It needs to stem from a sincere desire to be interested in others. In other words, this calls for being genuinely interested in people, as opposed to what they you can get from them. For your character to display warmth, it needs to stem from the core of your being – a good heart.

How do you Develop Warmth?

For the purpose of this book, we will discuss two major ways to develop warmth

Practice gratitude. To be truly happy and appreciate the finer things of life, you need to be grateful. This will, in turn, reward you with satisfaction with your life and the people around you. To develop gratitude, think about everything in your life that makes you happy. This will transform into a sense of contentment that will be seen in every department of your life and other people around.

Work on developing empathy. Empathy is very important for developing warmth. It is that desire in people to be understood, and empathy is the virtue that makes it possible. It is the ability to put ourselves in others' shoes and assume what they are going through.

See others as your siblings. It is assumed that billions of years ago, we all share the same parents, according to some religious belief. Thinking of everyone as a big family will go a long way in helping to be compassionate.

Prioritize face-to-face conversation. Seeing and interacting with people face to face, rather than online interaction can trigger empathy in humans.

When people annoy you, imagine a different story. It is easy to blame people when they do something wrong or when we feel trampled upon. Yet, we have a way of excusing ourselves and our character flaws when we do something wrong to others. Showing the same compassion that we showered on ourselves to others can go a long way in developing empathy.

Be genuinely interested in knowing people. There is no way you can understand what someone is going through without getting to know them. Ask questions and show genuine concern. A sincere interaction can help you learn something about someone and life in general.

Work on developing your empathy. It will help you realize that the people you meet as you go through life all have things they are struggling with. With this, you can develop an understanding spirit and attitude that lightens people up and make them feel understood.

Conveying Warmth to Others

When you convey warmth, people find solace in you. You are like a safe haven and a shoulder for them to cry on. They know that irrespective of their circumstances, you will make them feel comfortable and taken care of. It is however, important to work on developing warmth alongside other elements of charisma.

As emphasized above, if you display warmth to others, it must emanate from a sincere heart.

However, even if that is not the kind of person you are, you can take some steps to develop it, till it becomes part of you. If you want to work towards showing care to people, you can try the following behaviors. However, they must emanate from a sincere heart, unless people will see easily see pass the veil you are putting forward.

Offer a Sincere Compliment

Compliments have power. It can strengthen a relationship and even repair a bad one. As a result, quit being reserved with your words and look for ways you can make someone feel special. It will go a long way to make you feel good as well.

Let Your Voice Convey Warmth

Communication is not only about the words we use, but how our voice comes out. In other words, your tone, pitch and manner of speaking can all work together to communicate warmth. Take caregivers like a nurse for instance. They have a soothing way of making you feel that everything will be okay, that you can pull through – that is warmth. You can direct kindness to people with a soft tone accompanied with a smile. Imagine an air hostess for instance, I bet part of their training is how to smile and make passengers feel comfortable. You can emulate such in your interaction with people.

Mirror the Body Language

You want to build rapport with someone, appear pretty attractive, and establish trust? The best way is to mirror their body language. This creates a connection between both individuals that makes it possible to develop empathy.

In mirroring someone, match your tone with theirs and copy the position of their arms and legs. Watch how they are sitting on the chair and mimic it. If they lean toward you, follow suit. If they have their legs crossed, repeat it as well. It is, however, important not to make mirroring obvious. In fact, allow for a couple of seconds lapse before assuming the other person's position.

Give an Open Posture

The idea is to make you come off as approachable and willing to be a shoulder to cry on. You cannot appear approachable with a closed off body posture. Hence, be sure you always have a smile and avoid crossing either the hands or legs when with people. Remove barriers between you and the other person.

Always have a Smile

With a smile, you are not only conveying warmth but also giving yourself the opportunity to feel it. Smiling is harmless and costs you nothing. It can also lift your spirit to feel happy and warm even if you are not feeling like it. It can condition you for a warm mindset before you reach out to others.

Besides conveying warmth, smiling has a way of making you attractive. A smile signals that you mean no harm and you come in peace. This draws people to you and registers your good intention in their mind.

Anticipate Needs

In other words, do not wait for someone to ask. Be sensitive enough to know what someone might need and offer it. With this, it shows them you are a thoughtful and reliable personality. Even without asking, offer to help that grandma cross the road.

Make a cup of coffee or green tea and offer it to a sick colleague. The possibility of getting rejected is low.

Offer a Good Handshake

Handshake, besides hug is the most common avenue you have to make a skin to skin contact with another person, make it good. In offering handshake, make sure you are invested in it. Be sure to have a firm grip without exerting excessive pressure on the other person. Shake the hand for a couple of seconds and accompany it with a smile and an eye to eye contact. With the kind of handshake you give, people can deduce if you are keen on the interaction or not hence you have got to be mindful of how you give it.

Remember details about People

How amazing and special that feeling when people pour in their birthday wishes, people you don't even expect. It makes you feel special and loved. It is one of the simplest ways to show empathy. This, however, is not about writing on someone's Facebook wall. Pick up the mobile phone and put a call across, send a card. Do something thoughtful and stand out from the crowd. It is not about birthdays alone. Keep people's wedding anniversary in mind.

In addition to that, be sure to remember people's names and whatever it is they care about. Remember their kid's name and the name of the pet they care so much about.

Chapter 10
Positive Thinking

Negative thoughts can also lead to a very low self-esteem. People who get in the habit of thinking negatively about situations will eventually turn that negativity on themselves, blaming themselves and judging themselves for everything.

On the Flip Side: Positive Thinking

I know a lot of people who like to call themselves "realists." These people are, generally, pretty negative people. They always jump to the worst-case scenario, think the worst of others' motivations and intentions, and have the most negative view of themselves. But they're just "realists." People who are more positive are "idealists." And maybe a little naive, too.

of issues. They don't seek to avoid stress at all costs by glossing over all of their problems. Yes, there are some people who do that, but true positive thinkers acknowledge all of these things and still believe they can overcome it. They generally expect that good things will happen to them and that they'll have a pretty good life. They know that bad things will happen, but they know they will be able to overcome them.

Positive thinkers are much better equipped to handle the stresses of life simply because they believe in their ability to rise above. So instead of becoming frozen by negative thoughts, they search for solutions and are proactive about implementing them.

The way you think can become a self-fulfilling prophecy. Those who choose to think positively are naturally able to learn more, leading them to better successes and generally happier life. On the other hand, those who choose to wallow in negative thoughts tend to be paralyzed and unable to focus on anything besides the situation immediately in front of them.

How to Start Thinking Positively

1. Practice mindfulness

    o At the top of your lungs, play a game, read a book, build something. I know life is busy and it's difficult to find the time for something that doesn't feel productive, but if you can set aside ten minutes every day for something you love, it will be well worth it.

    o Mindfulness is a great way to train yourself to think more positively. Instead of going through all of your time on autopilot, take a few minutes every day to be keenly aware of your thoughts. Take every thought you have and ask yourself, "Is this a positive or a negative thought? If it's negative, why am I choosing to think negatively about this situation and how can I change my thoughts to be more positive?"

2. Keep a record of your thoughts

    o In this case, you have to become aware of your negative thoughts. To do this, start keeping a record of your thoughts and emotions. For a few days in a row, keep a small journal and a pen with you at all times. Every time you feel your emotions change throughout the day, write it down. Make a note of what was going on, the emotion you experienced, and what you were thinking during that time. Try your best to do this as soon as possible after a shift in emotions so you can have the most accurate record possible.

- o Later, during your time of self-reflection or meditation, ask yourself if the thoughts and emotions you had were helpful. If they weren't, take a few minutes to reflect on how you could avoid having those thoughts and emotions the next time something similar is happening.

3. Do something you love for at least 10 minutes a day

How You See Yourself

All in all, aren't certainty and confidence something very similar? Fundamentally the same as, truly, however not indistinguishable. There are some key contrasts.

At its most fundamental, confidence is simply the worth that you place inside the world. "Am I significant as an individual?", as such. Ideally, you would answer yes to that, which implies that your confidence would be high. As referenced, confidence doesn't will in general change after some time, since it is identified with how you see yourself.

In any case, certainty is identified with some demonstration. The conviction you can achieve something. It is, subsequently substantially more explicit than confidence. Along these lines, you could be certain that you are an incredible skier, however have no trust in your capacity to fly a plane.

It is a lot simpler to adjust your degree of certainty than it is to change your confidence. You can assemble certainty by rehearsing the movement you question your capacity at. For instance, you could take flying exercises, and as your expertise at controlling the flying machine increments, so will your certainty.

Obviously, there is an association between confidence and self-assurance. Those with high confidence are probably going to be sure, also. In any case, this isn't all inclusive. There are a lot of instances of individuals who are absolutely sure about their capacities in a single domain and have horrendous confidence in each other pieces of their lives.

This distinction is critical. Certainty is a lot simpler to work than confidence. An individual may never turn into the best on the planet at some movement that they question their fitness in, however with enough practice, they can, in any event, figure out how to play out the action sufficiently. The objective of this book is to enable you to construct your confidence by structure up your certainty.

At the point when an individual with low confidence is approached to list the things they are great at, that rundown will probably be very short, while the rundown of things they accept they are terrible freely likely be very long. In this way, what we will do in the accompanying parts is to discover in what you are really great at, and where your territories of chance untruth.

When we have decided those things, we will ace the things that you believe you could utilize enhancement for. In the long run, in the event that you are straightforward with yourself about your qualities and shortcomings, and you invest the push to make the upgrades you want, your confidence will start to improve.

However, as referenced, this requires absolute genuineness with yourself in regards to your shortcomings and your qualities. Not we all can take a reasonable self-evaluation. On the off chance that you end up puzzled anytime, don't hesitate to talk with your dear loved ones, with the individuals who realize you best and will give you genuine criticism.

Living with low confidence can be troublesome, however by following the means sketched out in the following parts, you will discover your certainty improving step by step and in the long run, you will manufacture a solid and positive picture of yourself.

Learning to Love Yourself

You will be put on the right track and guided through the process of getting into the right mindset, much increasing your chances of success. Whatever change you go through in your life, there are four main phases: realization, contemplation, changing, and assimilation the first phase is realization, because you cannot expect to achieve results if you do not know what it is that needs to be improved upon.

Many people who are unhappy with life are unhappy with themselves. They don't think that they measure up to the people around them, or what is expected of them. This is, of course, nonsense but a depressed person won't believe that. In order to overcome issues that you face with your personal self-esteem, sit in front of a mirror and look at yourself.

Observation

The point of the exercise is to show you that no one actually measures up to every standard and that some people who were born at a disadvantage can actually be proud and confident because they are happy inside. When you learn to be comfortable in the skin you're in, you begin to gain confidence and your self-esteem gets much better. You see yourself as a whole person and are able to move through life without letting other people's criticism touch you. It really is as simple as that.

Chapter 1 The Mirror Exercise

You are probably your worst enemy right now. Most people who are depressed and anxious find that the unhappiness comes from inside. Thus, look at yourself in the mirror. Are you the kind of person you would want as a friend? When you are depressed and it shows on the outside, the inside is going to automatically feel worse. Thus, you need to take action. Wash your face, clean your teeth, brush your hair and dress in reasonable clothes. Stop neglecting yourself because it doesn't help your cause at all. When you feel dowdy and you don't bother with yourself, you make yourself feel even worse. This is something you can do something about and you need to because you can't feel very good about yourself when all you do is neglect yourself. It's not about looks. It's about self-respect and when you start to build that up, then confidence is something that happens as a result. Of course, you can have a makeover of your hairstyle or do more to make yourself look great, but the first steps are yours and yours alone.

Get into a routine again because that routine serves a purpose. It gives you times to groom yourself, to eat properly, to sleep for the right amount of time and to get you out of the funk of depression being demonstrated in your life.

Chapter 2 Being Present

One of the usual responses to the question, "How would you make a child feel loved?" is, "I'd give that child undivided attention." We are usually so caught up in the "busyness" of our lives that we rarely focus on the needs of our inner child. So often we put all the should, have-to and responsibilities in our life first. When we do manage to spend time with the child (whether our inner child or an external one), often our minds are off in some distant place, thinking about a past event or worrying about the future. Consequently, even though we are physically there, the child does not feel our presence. One significant way to love your inner child is to be present, even if it is only for a few minutes each day. Just as focusing attention on a child even for a short time can have a powerful and lasting effect, so can a similar focus nourish your inner child? Whether meditating, gazing at a beautiful nature scene, or just noticing the feelings in your emotional or physical body, spending a short period of time being fully present each day can do wonders.

Chapter 3 Spending Fun Time

Another point people mention regarding loving a child is making time to do something the child finds enjoyable—a practice that also nurtures your inner child. This means setting aside time to do whatever would please your inner child, letting it know that it is a priority and that you are serious about establishing a new relationship. As you practice this you will begin to experience definite changes in your inner child's behavior and attitude. I know that for me taking time to do enjoyable things has had a particularly strong, direct effect on my life.

It is important when scheduling an activity for your inner child, that it doesn't have a particular goal, just that it be something fun and enjoyable. Do what you love to do for its own sake, not for the benefit you are going to derive from it later. You do not have to be good at this activity. Often as children we enjoyed certain activities but weren't as good at them as some prescribed ideal, so we stopped doing them. The important thing is that the activity feels good to you and that you can lose yourself in it. Ask yourself what activity might you begin or get back to. Does a smile come to your face when you think about being in nature, playing sports, or doing something adventurous like skydiving or rock climbing? Or does doing something quieter like reading or playing chess bring you joy? Does dancing, singing, or painting sound like fun? Even if you have never done it before, it is never too late to start.

Spending time with your inner child in any one of these playful, creative, or nurturing ways may require rearranging your priorities. If having a more loving relationship with your inner child and all the joy, aliveness, and creativity that it can potentially bring is a high priority for you then you will be willing to pay the price of eliminating or rearranging activities necessary to achieve this.

Communicate

It is also important to be aware of how we speak. Without realizing it, we often communicate to ourselves in derogatory phrases we learned from our family or society, using put-downs and tones of voice that inhibit the inner child. A powerful exercise for communicating with your inner child is to regularly write to her or him. Start off with something like, "What is going on for you?" or "What are you feeling about?" or just "What are you feeling?" Then let the words flow. You can respond, engaging in a dialogue, or just let the child speak freely. You will often be amazed at what comes out.

Chapter 11
Believe in Yourself

Developing a Stronger Sense of Self Leads to Self-Confidence

Knowing and respecting your goals and values is an important part of self-confidence. Unfortunately, it's all too common for people to set aside their authentic self in order to please others.

Here are some ideas to help you develop a stronger sense of self:

Become Comfortable with Being Alone

If you want to do something, don't wait for others to join you. Go to a movie, or to an event you're interested in. Being by yourself may even be more enjoyable because you can focus all your attention on what you're doing.

Set and Keep Boundaries

Be clear on what you will and will not do. If you're afraid of disappointing others, you may find yourself doing a lot of things you don't want to do.

Go Your Own Way

Don't be afraid to do your own thing even if it goes against what everyone else is doing.

Don't Compare Yourself to Others

We're all on different paths and different stages in our lives. While it's tempting to compare ourselves to others, remember that what you see or think is going on, is probably not the reality.

List Past Successes and Use Them To Your Advantage

Taking stock of our wins is an excellent way to build our confidence. Write down your successes and the things which you're especially proud of. Keep your list in a journal where you can review it regularly, and especially when you've suffered a setback or are feeling discouraged.

Another good practice is to keep a daily list of small wins. These aren't the big victories like promotions, awards, and milestones. These accomplishments can be as simple as staying on track with your diet, not losing your temper in a frustrating situation, and starting a new class.

When you're climbing a mountain and see how far you still have to go, it can be easy to forget how far you've already come.

Recording your accomplishments is an enormous confidence booster because it's a reminder that of how much progress you've made.

Get Feedback from Others

Constructive criticism is a valuable tool if we knowhow to accept it. If you're working on a project, or learning a new skill, knowing what you're doing right and where you need improvement will help you do a better job.

Be open-minded and don't be defensive when hearing from others. Remember you want to improve and that comes with time and effort.

Replace Negative Beliefs with Positive Ones

This is one of the most valuable skills you can master and will be invaluable in your confidence building journey so we're going to spend quite a bit of time on this topic.

Confronting negative thoughts can feel impossible. You start to make progress and your inner critic kicks in again and you lose your momentum. You may start to wonder if you'll always be paralyzed by negative thoughts. Don't worry, self-doubt is natural. But that doesn't mean that your inner critic will always be in control of your mind.

I just know I'm going to get fired!

I'm a terrible parent.

I'll be alone for the rest of my life.

We all have the occasional negative thought. But many people battle negative thinking constantly. They're bombarded with thoughts which all revolve around one thing: telling them how worthless they are.

There are ways to handle negative thinking in a healthy way. Learning how to handle negative thinking in a healthy way will allow you to take action and build self-confidence.

Our minds have a constant stream of thoughts running through them. Some of them are neutral, others are even pleasant. And of course, we have some that are negative. These negative thoughts aren't the real problem -it's the power we give them.

If you choose to believe your negative thoughts, they'll erode your self-confidence and even stop you from moving forward in your life.

Common Types of Negative Thoughts:

Assumptions

When you make assumptions, you're filling the unknown with undesirable outcomes. In reality, a number of good things are also possible. But your negative thoughts don't allow you to see those possibilities.

The "Shoulds"

When you start thinking about all the things you should have done, or you should be doing, you're comparing yourself unfavorably and deciding that you fall short. This attitude shakes your confidence and makes it harder for you to reach your goals.

Black-and-White / All or Nothing

Black-and-white thinkers (also known as all or nothing) believe that things are either all good or all-bad, there's never a happy medium. So, if you failed a test, you immediately think you're a failure. If you have a fight with your spouse, then the relationship is doomed.

But you can't place things into black and white categories and once you realize that, you'll be a lot happier. You'll no longer be worried about what you must or should do. You understand that there are "what if's" and "maybes", and that the all or nothing perceptions are all in your mind.

Catastrophizing

Shifting from making assumptions to imagining an all-out worst-case scenario is called catastrophizing. A failure becomes insurmountable and it's easy to lose sight of reality.

Can you see any of your negative thoughts on this list? It's a good idea to start recording the negative thoughts that pop into your head. Eventually, you'll be able to recognize a pattern.

When you write a negative thought down, ask yourself if it's true or not. Then list the evidence that supports either conclusion.

How to Eliminate Negative Thinking

Now that you are aware of your negative thoughts, you can start to break free of them. Don't get frustrated if you find it difficult at first. Let's review a few techniques to help you work through these nagging thoughts.

Reframe Your Negative Thoughts

The next time you work on dismantling a negative thought, ask yourself a couple of questions. Is this thought helpful? Is it helping me move toward my goals or is holding me back?

If that doesn't work, try to reframe the thought in a more positive way. If you think that you're stupid because you never learned how to swim, tell yourself that you're proud of yourself for taking the steps to gain a skill you've always wanted to have.

You can also reframe your feelings. If you feel anxious, tell yourself that you fell this way because you're about to do something that is important to you. Instead of anxiety, reframe your feelings as excitement.

Remove Your Attachment to The Thought

Instead of saying, "I'm a loser", switch it to "I'm having the thought that I'm a loser". This is an important distinction even if it seems like a small thing because you gain the perspective that you are not your thoughts.

Visualize your negative thought as a balloon and imagine it floating away. Continue with each new, negative thought and them all float away.

Another technique is to thank your mind. If you're worried that the plane you're on is going to crash, thank your mind for being concerned about your safety.

Avoid Generalizations

Watch out for absolute terms like "always", "never", "all", "none". These words usually indicate black-and-white thinking. Make your self-talk as balanced and specific as possible.

If you're thinking, "I always screw things up", change the thought to, "Sometimes things don't go the way I planned. Sometimes they do, and sometimes they even go better than expected".

Calm Your Inner Critic

You can't get rid of your inner critic, but you can learn how to keep it calm and take away its power. Give it a name like Negative Nancy. Remember that it has good intentions; it's trying to save you from potential failure or embarrassment.

Identify Your Negative Core Beliefs

Your core beliefs are the principles that guide you through life. They can be positive or negative. When they're self-limiting, they trick your mind into seeing the world as more dangerous than it is.

There are several common core beliefs, see if any of these resonate with you:

- I don't belong
- The world is dangerous
- I'm a failure
- I have to be perfect

- People can't be trusted
- Life is full of heartbreak and despair
- My needs aren't important

Chapter 12
Comfort Zones

The term "comfort zone" just sounds nice, doesn't it? It brings to mind a sanctuary where we're safe, taken care of and, well, comfortable. However, that imagery is deceiving. It tricks us into thinking that comfort zones are where we are supposed to be when, in reality; they're slowly draining the life from us.

To cultivate mental toughness, it's necessary to know what comfort zones are, how they work, and why we should ditch them as fast as we can.

What Is a Comfort Zone?

The general definition of a comfort zone is a psychological state in which your environment and routines promote feelings of safety and are devoid of anxiety or stress. An important thing to note, however, is that this doesn't translate to happiness necessarily. For a while, we may be content in comfort zones. After all, that's what they're there for. We may be with a partner we are reluctant to leave because we've become used to being with them, working a job that doesn't satisfy us but is "good enough," and living in a city that's strangling our potential but moving would be too big a change.

Comfort zones are those boxes or boundaries we put ourselves in that mental toughness helps us push past or climb over. You'll find out how soon.

Why We Have Comfort Zones

Simple: we crave safety. Back when we were living in the bush and half the animal kingdom wanted to eat us, comfort zones were physical places where we could let our guard down and relax for a short while. These may have been caves, camps, or small villages. Comfort zones were essentially safety zones, and in those days, that was just fine.

Enter the modern age. Comfort zones are no longer physical but psychological. We have taken the places that offered safety and put them in our minds, associating the lack of stress or anxiety with something positive. However, since the element of life or death is gone, comfort zones now act as limitations rather than an evolutionary advantage.

When something is new, different, or uncertain, it scares us. Our brains tell us that change is bad, and since our brains are usually right, we listen without question. Even if we feel a deep craving for something more, we stick to what we know to avoid pain. Comfort zones are survival mechanisms, but they're outdated.

How Your Comfort Zone Is Holding You Back

Here's the real problem with comfort zones: they put up barriers that separate you from your potential. It's like being in a city where all the propaganda is telling you is that life's great, but you can see through the chain-link fence to the other side and want to know what's out there. It takes courage to climb over or tunnel under that fence, and the longer you stay in your comfort zone, the less likely you are to try to escape.

Comfort zones stop us from realizing our potential and living our lives. We often settle in them because we feel like we have to be grateful for where we're at and that asking for more would be greedy. If you have a home, someone who loves you, and a good job, why upset the apple cart?

Because you'll never get where you want to be if you settle for "good enough."

Do you think Olympic athletes aim for second or third because they're almost first, and therefore close enough? Of course not. They aim to win. Every. Time. They reject comfort zones fully and completely. That's how they reach the top of their game.

It's time to do the same in your life. If you're still not convinced that comfort zones are actually killing your potential, consider some of these consequences that arise when you stick with what's safe and familiar:

- You don't get to find out your true strength because you never push your limits.

- Because you're always operating within the minimum requirements, you only see minimal results.

- You don't learn and grow. In 10 years, you'll be exactly where you are now because you won't gain the experience needed to progress.

- You forget what it means to truly live because you're stuck in the same routines that no longer serve you.

- You'll be afraid to do what you really want to do and thus ignore your inner calling.

- Once you realize your comfort zone is no longer comfortable, even the false sense of contentment will disappear. Unhappiness follows shortly after.

- You'll never reach your goals. They exist outside your comfort zone.

In the end, it's far more ungrateful to live a small life than to embrace every opportunity this vast world has to offer.

How Do You Know If You're Stuck in a Comfort Zone?

Sometimes, we don't even realize we're in a comfort zone until something happens that wakes us up, or we smack into the barrier that we didn't know was there. Comfort zones are sneaky; they can pop up when we're not paying attention and only make themselves known when a new opportunity on the other side of the fence comes along and we're too uncertain to take it. If you're not sure if you're trapped in your comfort zone, read over a few of the signs to help you decide.

You Feel Like You're Stuck in a Rut

This is basically just another way of saying you're in your comfort zone, but it's a phrase we're more familiar with and it stirs up a sense of discontent that actually makes it easier for you to break free. While "comfort zone" sounds positive, "stuck in a rut" does not. It makes us think that we're not going anywhere—because we're not.

You might feel like you've had the same routine for too long or that you're not making any progress. Maybe life has become predictable and dull. When you have this feeling, don't despair. It's a good thing because it shows a desire for change. Use that to push yourself forward out of the rut.

You Avoid Anything New or Different

It's natural to be uncomfortable in a new situation or when you're doing something out of the ordinary, but if even the idea of change, of something outside your routine, makes you panic, that's a bad sign. When you're unwilling to expand your horizons or stray away from what's familiar out of fear, you're hiding behind the supposed safety provided by your comfort zone. You convince yourself that you're avoiding danger, but in reality you're avoiding discomfort. Nonetheless, a little discomfort is good. It shows that you have room to grow.

Mentally tough people seek out new experiences because they're instructive. They know they won't grow or learn if they don't try something out of the ordinary and step away from what's familiar. This doesn't mean they're not afraid. It means they don't let the fear control them.

You Don't Remember the Last Time You Asked for or Received a Raise

It might seem unrelated, but one aspect of mental toughness is asking for what you deserve. If you're not doing that, something's wrong.

If you haven't received a raise in a while, it could be because your job performance hasn't increased (which indicates you're in your comfort zone of ease and are "coasting"), or possibly because you are afraid to ask and get a "no." There's nothing wrong with knowing your value and demanding it be met with the appropriate compensation. When you respect yourself and your talents, you won't accept any less from others.

If, on the other hand, your job performance is to blame, look at why that is. Are you bored with your job and don't want to put effort in because you're not inspired? Do you feel unappreciated and thus have less of a reason to work hard? Both of these problems can be solved only if you step outside your comfort zone. Ask for what you deserve, and don't be content with anything less.

You're Not Working Towards Any Goals

Your life should always have a purpose and direction. Otherwise, you're just drifting. If you don't have any goals, or you've let your goals fall by the wayside, you'll naturally settle into a comfort zone. When we don't have goals or direction, we tend to stay put or drift. This lack of forward momentum helps erect comfort zone barriers. If you've been in the same place long enough, you'll begin to want to stay there because moving is too difficult.

Goals provide avenues for progress and act as guides that lead you to the next level of your life. Without them, you won't know which way to go, and you'll end up not going anywhere.

You've Lived in the Same and City and Been with the Same Person for Years, But You Don't Know Why

This book isn't out to give you dating advice or tell you to leave your loving partner. However, there's a difference between being in a relationship because you want to and being in one because you don't want to not be in a relationship and/or it's familiar. The people we spend the most time with have the biggest impact in our lives. If you're not happy with your partner, you won't be happy with yourself.

The same idea goes for your job. If you love your job, you feel fulfilled, and there's opportunity for growth. Then, of course, you'll want to stay for years. If you haven't advanced and don't enjoy what you do anymore, but you're too afraid to switch careers or companies, then you've made a nice, cushy comfort zone around yourself that guarantees financial security but sacrifices well-being.

Mental toughness requires evaluation. It can sometimes seem harsh, but it's necessary. You need to ask yourself the right questions and be honest about the answer. Comfort zones often bring with them a touch of denial, but you're not doing yourself any favors by pretending you're okay with the way things are. Ask yourself the following questions:

- Is this job helping me further my career?
- Am I in a city with plenty of opportunities for me?
- Does this job fit my passion?
- Do I feel like my life is meaningful?
- Does this situation serve me and my goals?
- Have I outgrown this person/job/city?

If you answer 'no' or "I don't know," you have some thinking to do. You should always feel like you're in the right place, not the easy one.

You Feel Like You Were Meant for More

...but you're afraid to ask what that "more" is. Although almost all of us have felt this at some point, how many of us listen to that call from within? We can still hear it when we're in our comfort zones, but we try to ignore it and bury it deeper. We feel like it's asking too much, especially if we already have lives that look successful. You can have a great job, beautiful house, fancy car, and thousands in the bank and still live within a comfort zone.

You're allowed to ask for more from life. That's what your entire existence is for! Not settling, not striving for "good enough," not giving up, and accepting that content must mean happy, even if it doesn't feel like it.

Mental toughness gives you the push needed to follow the call that tells you there's more out there for you. If you feel like you were meant for greater things, you are.

Strategies for Getting Out of Your Comfort Zone

It can be disheartening to realize that you've constructed walls around your life that stop you from pursuing what you truly want. That's not the end of the story, though. Now that you know you're in one, you can learn how to break out of your comfort zone. You don't have to leave it behind entirely or all at once, but start to test your limits and see how far you can push yourself. It won't be easy, of course. You'll need to learn how to deal with the stress that comes from taking chances and leverage resilience and discipline to keep you going when you want to quit.

For now, consider some of the following strategies to start pushing past the limitations you've set for yourself and break free.

Do What Scares You

This is perhaps the easiest and hardest way to escape your comfort zone. Anything that scares you is 100% outside your comfort zone because nothing in it stirs up feelings of fear, hence the comfort part.

So, what scares you? Are you afraid of asking for a raise? What about moving to a new city or even just a new neighborhood? Are you too nervous to ask out the person you've been eyeing at the coffee shop? Remember that mental toughness naturally involves a little fear, but overcoming that fear is what makes you tougher.

Start small and pick something that won't have massive repercussions. For instance, you're afraid to speak up in a meeting because you don't think your ideas will be accepted or appreciated. Do it anyway. What's the worst that can happen?

No one listens. What's the best that may happen? Your boss finally sees that underneath that fear is a brilliant mind that's ready to handle bigger and better opportunities. Just like that, you're on a new trajectory because you have looked fear in the face and said, "Move over."

Change an Ordinary Routine in a Small Way

When your habits revolve around your comfort zone, they're anything but helpful. When we have the same old routine day after day, life starts to feel extremely dull. Counteract this by making one small change, even if it's too small it seems insignificant.

Do you go to the same coffee shop every morning? If so, go somewhere else. Do you make the same dinner or meal all the time? Then, find a new recipe and give that a try. What about your route to work? Is that always the same? Grab your GPS and look for a different route to get there.

All of these things add up to create a significant effect because they snap you out of autopilot and let you really experience the world around you. Once you do, you'll realize what you've been missing by clinging to what's familiar.

Try One New Thing You've Always Wanted to Try

This ties into doing what scares you, but there's meant to be more of a reward attached to it. Most of us have list upon list detailing all the things we want to do, from skydiving to traveling the world. The sad part is, we never do any of these things because we're too busy 'living' (see: settling).

Take a pottery class. Go to Germany. Learn to SCUBA dive. Get a dog. Stop adding to that list—in fact, tear it up. Instead of writing something down for later, do it right then and there. If you wait for the time to be right, especially when you're still in your comfort zone, you'll never do it. There's no room for anything new within your self-imposed boundaries, so get out of them.

Say Yes to Something You've Said No to in the Past

Often, when we're in our comfort zone, our knee-jerk reaction is to say no. Saying no means that we're safe and that we don't run the risk of encountering an unfamiliar situation. This isn't always the case, of course. 'No' is sometimes necessary when we're genuinely concerned for our safety or feeling overburdened. However, the vast majority of the time, 'no' simply means "I'm afraid to say yes." Don't be afraid. Do it.

If a friend asks you to go to a ballroom dancing class, say yes.

If your kids ask you to take them to the park, but you have work to do, drop the work. Say yes. They'll only be young for so long.

When the barista asks if you want whipped cream on your coffee, definitely say yes.

It's not about mindlessly agreeing, it's about learning how 'yes' feels compared to 'no.' Saying yes to the little things is like saying yes to life.

Getting Comfortable Being Uncomfortable

I know I've spent a lot of time talking about changing the things in your life that you've felt comfortable with. When you decide to actively pursue your dreams, you have to do something that many of us struggle with. You have to get comfortable being uncomfortable.

What's that supposed to mean?

It means that being uncomfortable will become a fact of life as you continue to follow your dreams and push your limits. Once you get to a place where you feel comfortable with the changes you're going to make, you'll have to leave your comfort zone again.

The thing about pushing your limits and following your dreams is that it's an ongoing process. Human beings are adaptable. When we try something new, it's uncomfortable at first, but with the passage of time it becomes more comfortable. This often happens before we have reached our goals.

If you want to follow your dreams and actively pursue your vocation, you must be prepared to continue expanding your comfort zone.

Personal growth occurs outside your comfort zone.

So, in order to continue to pursue your dreams, you must make the decision to feel comfortable with the discomfort. As soon as you decide that you are well with the discomfort, you will be able to leave your comfort zone much more easily.

This doesn't mean you don't feel uncomfortable. It just means you won't react negatively every time you do. You'll be prepared for it and better able to handle it.

I can speak from experience. It's not an easy thing to do, but it's extremely necessary. Pursuing your vocation or life purpose is a long-term effort.

The journey to a successful life is a marathon, not a career. You have to be in it for the long haul. This means that you must be prepared to set goals, reach those goals and exceed your comfort zone many times throughout your life.

The best way to feel comfortable being uncomfortable is to do it in stages. While there are some people who can jump into the cold, frozen pool and adjust to temperature in one fell swoop, others prefer to submerge their feet slowly.

I'm going to give you the slow approach, but if you're one of those who get into it, I encourage you to do it too.

Ultimately, you have to do what's best for you.

1. Create a vision board of the goal you would like to achieve.

You can create a complete board or simply publish an image of the objective you would like to achieve in a visible place. You want to be able to see her regularly. Putting a picture you often see will help make the goal more real in your mind.

Goals can often seem like faraway things that we hope to achieve someday. The vision board or photo makes it less distant.

2. Do something you've never done before.

Find something you've never tried and give it a chance. You can start small and try a type of food you've never eaten or you can try a dish you've never tasted. As you become more comfortable with the smaller things, look for other things you can try and then try them.

3. Play the "what if" game.

Do this with someone close to you who doesn't mind asking the hard questions. Ask each other a series of "what if" questions about your life and be prepared to answer them honestly.

If necessary, record the questions and your answers. It is helpful to keep a record of these questions for later review. You have to say the answers instead of writing them down. We tend to edit words that we write much more than we say.

We all create comfort zones as a form of personal security. It allows us to be comfortable in our skin and carry out our daily lives with relative ease. It takes work to get out of your comfort zone, but it must happen if you want to pursue your dreams.

Your comfort zone is a mental creation, which means that in order to get out of it, you must change your thoughts. It's not easy to change the way you think. I just shared a few things that will help you get started in that process.

Opening your mind to other possibilities makes it easier to accept that you can achieve goals that may seem distant and impractical. It makes it possible to believe that you have the ability to change your life.

Remember, personal growth occurs outside YOUR COMFORT ZONE.

Chapter 13
Leveraging Your New Self-Esteem

Anxiety and depression. Illnesses, or conditions of our time. Why? Is it the stress that we are subjected to, with 24-hour-a-day news informing us of the violence, poverty, illnesses and diseases, accidents and natural catastrophes that occur, seemingly nonstop? These events and situations are hardly new to our time, but never before have we become so aware, so continuously. In addition, is it the stress that is induced by politics, which appear to have become more polarized, more tumultuous, and more confrontational and emotional today? Is it concern over global warming and the long-term threats to our planet and its populations? Do you envision ever-stronger hurricanes, melting glaciers and icebergs, and sinking coastlines?

Yes, all of these world-affecting events and situations can contribute to frustration, confusion, anger, disorientation, and other states of mind. The net emotional reaction is stress. But, in most cases, the stress that leads us to anxiety and depression, insecurity, and feelings of inferiority is from what is perceived and reacted to from within, not from outside world events, even if these ongoing conditions do have some degree of impact upon us emotionally.

Self-Esteem to Overcome Anxiety

Stress is a primary cause of anxiety and can be created by a number of events or situations that affect us on a personal basis. Stress at work can occur at every level of responsibility, whether you are a teaching assistant at a high school or the school's principal. You can be a trainee in your first job or the chief executive officer of a large corporation. Your work can be grilling burgers at a fast-food restaurant or teaching university level nuclear physics. Nobody is exempt from the stress that may be caused by their work; stress creates anxiety.

The stress may be in response to time pressures and deadlines, criticism of the quality of your work, an inability to show up on time, distractions to your work caused by family or personal issues, or it may be that your authority is being challenged, whether it's by students or by subordinates. In these two extreme examples, imagine a teacher who cannot control the students or maintain discipline or decorum, or consider a military officer or a sergeant not gaining the respect and obedience from the troops that their rank and authority deserves.

If you are a student, the pressure of your studies and exams can combine with tension or discomfort with other students, with teachers or professors, leading to stress that makes it hard to study, to learn, and to handle your exams. Just the exams themselves can create stress that leads to anxiety, because you are being challenged on what you have learned, on how well you can express it, and whether you can get your preparation for the exam completed in time. Students are generally required to become knowledgeable of a number of diverse subjects at the same time, and few of us are competent across all categories of knowledge. Stress to students can be exacerbated by the myriad social pressures that arrive with the onset of adulthood, including attracting potential companions and the so-called "rating and dating" complexities of youth.

Your personal life can also generate stress, especially when things are not going well in a relationship. This can be as simple, and as short-term, as not having your calls or texts responded to favorably, or not being responded to at all. Or, it can involve a marriage in difficulty, which can become a prolonged, painful, and upsetting experience. Your friends and associates may create stress, perhaps unintentionally, by virtue of their achievements, whether they are academic, vocational, financial, or social, creating in you a feeling of inadequacy. The stress from any of these causes can lead to a condition of anxiety. In cases like the marriage problems, the stress-induced anxiety can continue for years, leading to physical as well as psychological problems.

The physical problems induced by anxiety may include fatigue, muscular weakness, and a state of provoking the sympathetic nervous system's fight or flight response, meaning a person cannot relax, and their heartbeat, breathing rates, and blood pressure levels are elevated, with additional surges of energy-inducing hormones.

The hormonal infusions, in turn, can make changes in how the immune system responds to infections, leading to a greater susceptibility to illness.

Others may experience insomnia, and the resultant sleep deprivation can intensify the state of anxiety. Many anxiety sufferers also experience digestive disorders, including diarrhea, gastric upset, acid indigestion, and the more serious acid reflux, ulcers, and gastroesophageal disorder. Other anxiety-related disorders include excessive sweating, jitteriness, and loss of sex drive.

Clearly, anxiety is not a condition that should be allowed to continue as it disrupts the quality of life and can lead to long-term physical damage.

If the anxiety is extreme or long-lasting, medical treatment should be sought. However, in many cases, the stress that is causing the anxiety can be reduced or eliminated by building self-esteem and raising self-confidence. Reactions to stress and the onset of anxiety can be blunted or diverted by stronger self-esteem.

Begin with recognizing the causes of anxiety, such as the pressures at work or during your education or the frustrations you may feel from the successes and competencies of others. If you are shy, acknowledge that this started early in your life and does not have to continue to hold you back. Push yourself to become conversant, to engage with others.

Confront the sources of your anxiety and find ways to diffuse them and you will have taken a major step towards taking control of your life and managing your reactions. There are instructions on exercise, yoga stretches, managed breathing, and meditative self-control. These physical and mental actions can create further, tangible progress in building your ego, your self-esteem, and your self-confidence, and raising a protective wall around you, reducing stress and diminishing anxiety.

If anxiety creates a surge of energy and activity, the opposite can occur when someone experiences depression, which is generally accompanied by an overall slowdown in bodily functions and initiative.

Self-Esteem to Overcome Depression

Caveat: This is important. Depression can be a serious, life-threatening condition, or it may be less severe, yet still able to affect and diminish the quality of life. It is important to recognize that medical professionals best treat the severe, chronic, and deeply troubling forms of depression. Some serious forms of depression may be resolved through psychotherapy, while drugs may be prescribed to supplement the therapy. Severe depression should not be ignored, as it may lead to feelings of hopelessness and desperation, suicidal thoughts, or worse. Severe, debilitating depression is frequently caused by chemical or hormonal imbalances and can be effectively diagnosed and treated.

Get help immediately. If you feel you are deeply depressed and may be having thoughts of hurting yourself or committing suicide, *seek immediate help* by dialing 911 or going to a hospital emergency room. Depression is a real condition that may need professional help; so do not feel embarrassed or ashamed to reach out for support.

For our purposes, this discussion concerns common, non-severe depression that we all may experience from time to time. We may define this form of depression as unhappiness, a negative sense of expectation, and possibly a continuing belief that things probably will not work out for the best. Symptoms of even moderate depression may include fatigue or feeling lethargic, a feeling of uselessness, excessive worrying, and anticipated bad outcomes. A depressed person cannot manage to embrace the good aspects of life to offset the negative aspects. They are unable to shake off what may feel like a shadow over them or a weight pressing down.

Other common symptoms of depression include a loss of appetite, either sleeping too much or too little, a feeling that you are worthless, feeling guilty about something that may not have any relevance, and difficulty keeping one's mind on track or be able to concentrate and see projects to conclusion. A professional diagnosis of depression requires continued symptoms for at least two weeks.

Depression may result in causing both physical and emotional problems and can reduce functional capabilities and competencies at work, in various activities and among family and friends at home. Depression is distinguished from grief and sadness associated with a personal loss, but prolonged grief can induce a condition of long-term depression.

Depression can affect anyone at any time in their lives but is most likely to first appear among teens and young adults. It tends to occur more frequently among women than among men, and some studies show that one-third of women will experience depression at least once in their lives. Overall, at some time in their lives, depression can affect between 6% and 7% of the population, which is one person in 15.

Fortunately, depression is one of the most treatable mental disorders, with an 80% to 90% success rate. Professional treatments for depression include medication, such as antidepressants, which modify chemical disorders in the brain. Psychotherapy, which involves the patient talking through issues with the therapist, can be effective, but in some cases, it is performed in addition to medication. Cognitive behavior therapy (CBT) has been successful in helping people recognize distorted thinking, leading to attitudinal and behavioral modifications.

Self-esteem and overcoming depression. It is possible to treat milder forms of depression with self-help methods that build self-esteem and raise self-confidence. These approaches include all of the methods we've been discussing generally: cardiovascular and resistance types of exercise, yoga stretching, meditation, mindfulness, and managed breathing.

If you feel you are depressed, especially if negative thoughts are prevailing, you find yourself lying awake at night, unable to sleep, or if you're just not "feeling yourself," a good routine of exercises and mind-influencing steps can get you back on track. To optimize the effects of whatever routine you follow, insert positive thinking into the rhythmic breathing, saying to yourself, "I am successful, I am positive, I am optimistic, I can do anything," or any other positive, uplifting words that you believe define the best part of you and give you inspiration that life is good and that you are good and getting better.

Give your exercise and meditative routines a chance to work for you. Perform these actions every day, ideally at the same time each day, which will increase the likelihood that you will not skip days. Do not make excuses for missing your self-help practices, and never allow yourself to think "I don't have time," which is simply an excuse for avoidance or a lack of motivation.

Depression, and its related negativity and sense of frustration with one's self, may be brought on by feelings of insecurity. These self-defeating thoughts, and their resultant inferiority complex, may be induced, surprisingly, by others with feelings of insecurity. These types of people try to build themselves up by impressing you with their prowess and making you feel lesser in comparison. The following section will show you how to recognize when you are being intimidated and how to counter it, raising your self-esteem in the process.

Self-Esteem to Overcome Insecurity

There are many causes of anxiety and depression, which are common conditions among many people today. While stress has been identified as a primary culprit, in reality, insecurity and uncertainty are of relevance in allowing or permitting stress to take hold in the first place. So, if someone is insecure, they have no natural defense against the taking hold of stress, of causing panic, of triggering the sympathetic nervous system's infamous fight or flight reaction, and thus accelerating and exacerbating the symptoms of anxiety and stress.

Strengthening self-esteem is the key to creating the mental armor that enables us to manage stress, keeping it from taking control of mood, diminishing our resolve and threatening our quality of life and mental and physical health.

So, what exactly is insecurity?

It derives from the Latin word *insecurus* and is generally defined as feeling unsafe and lacking self-confidence, and as a form of anxiety caused by a weak sense of self. Interestingly, some insecure people can present a facade, seeming to be a perfect, enviable person. This is actually a defense mechanism, and their objective in appearing so perfect is to make themselves more secure by making other people feel insecure.

For example, you encounter an acquaintance who informs you that her children are at the top of their classes, her husband is making a fortune, and she has started a blog that has close to a million visitors. You note that her appearance is impeccable. This may be entirely true, but it is more likely not an accidental revelation on her part, rather a well-defined behavioral pattern exhibited by an insecure person to make others feel insecure.

This behavior was identified by the Viennese pioneering psychoanalyst Alfred Adler, who developed the term "inferiority complex." Adler believed that people who feel inferior or insecure could adopt a series of behaviors that overcompensate for their sense of insecurity in what he termed "striving for superiority." They make themselves happy by making other people unhappy, and they try to achieve that by making people envious of them, even if the persona they project is an exaggeration. Modern psychologists now define this striving for superiority as a form of narcissistic personality disorder (NPD).

In trying to elevate your own self-esteem, it is important not to become overwhelmed or intimidated by these narcissistic types of people. They can damage whatever progress you are making in building your self-esteem and self-confidence. The best defense is to become aware of their behavior, be alert to it, and ignore it by reminding yourself that you are good, effective, and competent, and are immune to the falsified "act" that someone is putting on to feel better by diminishing you.

How to recognize people who try to cause insecurity and your solution:

Do some people make you feel insecure when you are around them? If you're generally comfortable with most people, but you recognize that a few, maybe just one, seem to make you question your own self-worth when you are with them, there's a good chance that you're in the presence of someone who is intimidating you deliberately. Do not let them question your own self-worth. Recognize that this person is trying, either consciously or subconsciously, to make themselves feel better at your expense.

Solution: Deflect the urge to feel bad and feel great about yourself. Recognize that this person is puffed up, full of hot air, and not to be envied.

Is someone you are with prone to bragging about their possessions or their accomplishments? Perhaps they are "borrowing" authority and value by bragging about someone else that they are close to. For example, imagine you recently completed a 10k running competition, and while the person you are talking with does not run at all, he is quick to point out that his neighbor completed the same run at a much faster time than yours.

Solution: Ignore the braggart and keep your pride and self-esteem intact. Be proud of your accomplishments.

Does the person act humble, while actually bragging? This technique might involve the person says they are feeling badly that they have to go out of town on a business trip, but they manage to work into the conversation that they're flying first class, staying in a suite at a top rated hotel, and are booked for dinner at a world-class restaurant. Other scenarios might include dropping the names of famous people they'll be meeting with.

Solution: Don't be impressed, you have better going on than this show-off. Whether the other person is telling the truth or not, realize that it's an effort to feel important at your expense.

Is the person frequently complaining that things are not good enough, to give the impression that they have a higher standard than everyone else? You think the movie you saw or the restaurant or the office or the museum is quite nice, while the other makes you think you have a low set of expectations.

Solution: Recognize that it's nonsense. Don't be drawn into this underhanded bit of bragging and keep your self-esteem and your dignity by deflecting the haughty attempt at superiority.

Conclusion

The book has covered rather a lot of territory and you may find that you need to go back to square one again and work on the exercises I have shared with you. Get to know yourself, get to love yourself and make a difference to the way in which the world sees you. It really does make a difference.

Once upon a time, I thought that I had no friends because I was defective in some way. That followed me all the way through my childhood. However, what I learned from the lessons in my life was that I had closed myself off to relationships and had thus not really encouraged friendship at all.

It was nothing to do with who I was or how defective I was at all. It was simply that the Law of Attraction was not drawing positive people into my life because I spent my time being negative. There are several others pointers I can give you to help you to get rid of negativity and these are:

Be in the moment whenever bad thoughts happen. Pull yourself into the reality of your life rather than the perceived reality. None of the stuff you are putting into your mind is real. It's all something fabricated by the mind. Inner happiness and peace are things that are really stable things that stay with you.

They also help you to be stronger when things go wrong in your life. You must learn that you are strong enough to deal with all of the problems in life in your own way and in your own time, instead of leaning on others to try and make up for any deficiency you perceive yourself to have. You are whole and complete and the only person on Earth that can begin to take that away from you is yourself.

Compassion is a wonderful thing and when you feel it in your life, it enriches it. Don't forget to remind yourself every day how important you are and all of the things that surround you that make you grateful to be you. I look sometimes into the pages of my journal and I see poetry I wrote years ago when I didn't like myself very much. It's like looking at the work of a stranger. I don't actually remember feeling that way at all, although I know that I must have.

When you find self-respect and self-love, what comes as a side product is self-compassion. Forgive yourself for not understanding it straight away and continue to work toward that aim because it's well worth it.

Remember you act as a magnet for the people in your life, but can only attract those people who are worthy of friendship by being worthy as a friend. You have the opportunity of your life lying ahead of you. Drop the suitcases from the past. They don't matter anymore because by now, you will have forgiven others and will have learned to forgive yourself.

As you walk toward the future, remember that you greet the world in a positive way with compassion and lack of judgment and everything changes. Life becomes rich and varied. It becomes challenging in all the right ways and you see your own potential and can share that with people who matter to you. This is when compassion is at its best. That's why I wrote this book. I got there and so can you.

When I woke up one morning feeling happy about who I was and how my life was treating me, suddenly the sun inside my soul started to shine. Yours can too.

I hope this book was able to help you to start realizing your real worth, embracing it, and loving yourself, as you deserve.

Made in United States
Orlando, FL
31 January 2024